50 Years of Photographing Hollywood
THE HURRELL STYLE

Photographs by George Hurrell

Text by Whitney Stine

The John Day Company

New York

*This book is affectionately dedicated to
all those Beautiful People*

Hurrell

Library of Congress Cataloging in Publication Data

*Hurrell, George.
    The Hurrell style.*

*Includes index.
    1. Glamour photography. 2. Hurrell, George.
I. Stine, Whitney, 1930–   II. Title.
TR678.H87   770'.92'4 [B]   76-15396
ISBN 0-381-98293-9 (H)
        0-381-98299-8 (P)
                2 3 4 5 6 7 8 9 10*

*Title page photograph: Hurrell with his Eastman Studio 8 x 10 portrait camera, 1931.
Preceding page: Advertisement for Hurrell's Sunset Boulevard studio.*

Contents

First Shots

Ramon Novarro poses at Poncho Barnes's estate in San Marino. 1928.

In 1925 Laguna Beach was little more than an art colony, situated on a few scenic bluffs sixty-four miles south of Los Angeles. Late in May of that year, a Hudson touring car, bearing Illinois license plates, glided smoothly along South Coast Highway and finally paused on a hilltop overlooking Emerald Bay. Painter George Hurrell and his companion, landscape artist Edgar Payne, climbed out of the car and made their way through the eucalyptus trees overlooking Sugarloaf Point.

Hurrell drew in his breath at the picture-postcard view below. The very atmosphere spelled youth, romance, and artistic freedom. The hot California sun, the mild Santa Ana breezes, and the crashing surf would provide the necessary inspiration to begin a career in the art world, and the climate would assuredly improve his health, recently impaired by a stubborn streak of bacteria.

An old wooden studio with the requisite skylight was promptly leased. (He learned later it was the birthplace of movie director Mal St. Clair.) Payne began a series of seascapes, and Hurrell sought out a local doctor on Forest Avenue, who gave him a sackful of pills the size and color of robin's eggs.

Besides a stack of empty canvases, an array of brushes, dozens of tubes of paint, and several cans of turpentine, Hurrell had also brought along an old Verito diffusion lens and a broken-down view box set atop a tripod that continually flew out from under it. Although envisioning himself as a painter, he had learned how to develop photographic negatives and make contact prints in Chicago while studying with the famous Midwest photographer Eugene Hutchinson. Barely out of his teens, Hurrell felt he knew all there was to know about photography.

He was an enthusiastic, brash extrovert, with a shock of unruly blue-black hair. He strode up and down Victoria Beach, dropped in for coffee at the modest studios of newly acquired friends, and informed all and sundry that he had a few finished canvases for sale. For a modest fee, he would also photograph paintings for art-magazine reproduction and take portraits of the local citizenry (twelve 8 x 10 films; one negative; three contact prints, mounted, for $20).

With much competition, he sold very few paintings. But his photography business flourished. Because he could not afford arc lamps, he continually experimented with the use of natural light and achieved striking effects using only the sunlight that filtered down from the skylight. The lessons learned in Laguna Beach were well put to use a few years later when he became the most sought after—and the most expensive—photographer in Hollywood. He would become famous for his use of light and shadow.

Hurrell conquered the elusive bacteria and saved his money. During the next eighteen months, he became acquainted with the "summer people" from San Bernardino, Riverside, and the desert communities, who owned the picturesque cottages that peppered the hillsides meandering down to the sea. Laguna was also awash with "summer widows" who took a romantic view of the intense young man who shot such interesting photographs.

His most staunch supporter was one of his first subjects, Florence "Poncho" Barnes, an unconventional socialite-aviatrix. Incongruously married to a minister from San Marino, she was famous for a Tailspin Tommy derring-do in the air, and for a wild collection of friends, indiscriminately gathered from local air circuses, Pasadena society, and the film colony. Hurrell and she shared many of the same qualities: both were "on stage" a great deal; both genuinely liked people; both were uninhibited, animated, and gregarious; both preferred the casual to the formal. In short, they were kindred spirits. Poncho, a handsome brunette woman, felt that Hurrell had not only captured a basic essence in her portraits—that certain reckless spirit for which she was known—but more importantly, a less recognized feminine quality that was not always apparent in her slapdash newspaper photographs.

A new housing development was slated for the acreage where Hurrell's studio was located and the owner, impressed with Hurrell's growing reputation, offered to move his studio building down the hill to a less populated area. Hurrell had packed his equipment and notified the utility companies to cut off the telephone, gas, and electricity, when artist William A. (Billy) Wendt asked him to go to Pasadena to photograph a gala that his wife was giving that same evening. Hurrell returned near midnight, lighted a few candles, developed his films, and was washing the prints when a familiar automobile horn beeped from a nearby grove of eucalyptus. He raced down the hill to his latest summer widow. A short time later, he looked up to find the studio in flames. Over the protestations of the volunteer fire department, Hurrell rushed into the building and barely managed to save two lenses, a camera, and a tripod. Billy Wendt took him in for the night.

Hurrell moved down the hill to another studio, and with the last of his meager savings, bought more secondhand equipment. Poncho, who admired his paintings but had a hunch that his real acclaim would come from the camera lens, helped him get back on his feet by further introductions to socialite friends who needed new photographs. Between sittings, he prowled Dana Point, sunned himself at Main Beach, took photographs of Moss Point, and explored the caves above Hidden Valley. But he was overcome with impatience; he was driven with a desire for change—a restless urge that would later take him back and forth between Hollywood and New York where he established several studios. His great physical energy was awesome.

During the autumn months of 1927, tourist trade declined to an alarming degree, and since Hurrell was working a great deal in Los Angeles, it seemed propitious to move into the city. He found a studio at 672 Lafayette Park Place—a tiny townhouse, in a garden court, with a modest room on the first floor and cramped living quarters above. He had acquired two arc lamps, and since he had no light meters, developed a keen instinct in timing, counting under his breath while making exposures. He continued to photograph the Pasadena social crowd as well as shoot the paintings of his artist friends for magazine reproduction. One such friend was Leon Gordon, who asked him one day if he would like to meet Edward Steichen, at that time the dean of American photographers, who was in town taking movie-star portraits for *Vogue* magazine. Steichen's reputation was so great that instead of going to the studio galleries to photograph the players, they came to his suite at the Ambassador Hotel where he had set up a camera and a few lights.

Meeting the legend was a momentous occasion. "Steichen's attempt to admire some of my own prints was indeed a kindness," Hurrell recalls. "But when I apologized for the size of my darkroom, which had once been a lavatory, he smiled and made two remarks that became the standards by which I have worked ever since *'Some of the best films I ever made were developed under a rug,'* he said. And *'Never let your subject know when you are baffled. Shoot the film anyway; make your change on the next shot—but be the master of the situation at all costs.'* "

Steichen then asked Hurrell to develop some films for him. They turned out to be not the expected movie-star shots, but a commercial job on a popular product, The Cigarette Lighter, commissioned by an advertising agency. "The Great Man stood in the dimness of my 2 x 4 darkroom," relates Hurrell, "while I developed the negs in a tray and made contact prints. I later discovered that he charged $1,500 for the three shots chosen by the agency. I was receiving about $40 for three contact prints at that time, and I was shocked. Then it dawned on me what enormous sums could be made from commercial photography."

Poncho Barnes and her plane, *Mystery Ship*, which she flew in and out of Mines Field, were making headlines. Between breaking speed records, she frequently dropped by Lafayette Park Place. One day, dressed in riding clothes, she arrived in her usual breathless condition and announced triumphantly: "I've got a big surprise! I've just met Ramon Novarro, and he wants some new portraits." She was flushed and excited, and Hurrell recognized the symptoms of a new romance.

"I'm very flattered," he exclaimed, "but, frankly, why doesn't he go to the studio photographer?"

"Oh, the sitting must be very hush-hush," she confided. "You see, it's not very well known, but he has a great operatic voice. He's going to make his concert debut in Vienna, but doesn't want M.G.M. to know about it quite yet. If he went to Ruth Harriet Louise at the studio, the prints would be circulated all over the lot."

That evening, Hurrell sat alone in the darkened studio, looking glumly at the bare walls and makeshift equipment. His earlier excitement had faded; he felt strangely depressed. One of the most famous movie stars in the world was coming to be photographed in a studio that was smaller than a dressing room at Metro-Goldwyn-Mayer.

Ramon Novarro

The sports roadster drew up before Hurrell's studio and a dark young man jumped out and opened the door for a woman in trousers and goggled cap. Hand in hand they bounded up the walk to the entrance of the court. "I've been wanting you two to meet ever so long," Poncho said breathlessly: "George Hurrell, this is Ramon Novarro."

Novarro extended his hand. "My friends call me 'Pete.' Now, where do I change?" Hurrell nervously pointed to the stairs.

"I've got to run down to Mines Field," Poncho laughed. "I'm due to meet some new pilots. After all those society dames you've been shooting recently, you'll have a great time with Pete. He's not at all the usual Hollywood type."

Novarro was one of the busiest stars at M.G.M. After playing the title role in *Ben Hur* in 1925, which consumed six months, and as many millions, to film, he was granted a long sabbatical, during which he resumed singing lessons. In 1927 he had three major films in release: *Lovers* with Alice Terry, *The Student Prince* with Norma Shearer, and *The Road to Romance* with Marceline Day. The last film had been released in October concurrently with the Warner Bros. film version of *The Jazz Singer* with Al Jolson. The Jolson vehicle was creating the first chilling currents that would sweep into the hurricane force about to envelop all of Hollywood:

sound! The Jazz Singer, filmed silently, contained musical numbers as well as a few lines of spoken dialogue. If "talkies" were truly in the offing, Novarro felt secure; he had a pleasant speaking voice, almost devoid of accent, and he could sing. He was prepared to bridge the gap between silent and sound pictures.

Although Hurrell did not expect Novarro to come charging down the staircase driving a chariot as he had in *Ben Hur*, he was, nevertheless, taken aback at the figure standing quietly on the landing. Novarro was dressed as a Spanish grandee and wore a huge silver ornamented sombrero. A freshly glued moustache was stuck none too securely to his upper lip. It was a dramatic moment. Novarro paused, head held high, then pointed to his costume. "Everyone takes me for a Spaniard, but I was born in Durango, Mexico. My real name is Samauiegos. But I am afraid that would not look very good on a marquee."

Hurrell posed him, arms over the back of a chair. "I set up my arc lamps," he remembers, "and found that Pete had photographically perfect features. And he could face my camera with a blank expression. Not at all like some of the men-about-town whom I had been photographing. I had to trick them into losing their solemn expression in order to get an interesting shot, but Pete was relaxed.

"I put a classical recording on the Victrola and he became more responsive. Pete, I discovered, was at his very best in left profile, or three-quarter front view. After the fourth or fifth exposure, I knew that I was catching something very appealing. Pete made many costume and

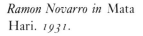

Ramon Novarro in Mata Hari. *1931.*

wig changes that first day and was not nearly ready when Poncho came back. Two days later, his face lighted up when he returned the proofs.

" 'You have caught my moods exactly,' he said. 'You have revealed what I am inside.' "

More movies were added to Novarro's slate and the concert tour was postponed again and again, but he continued to rehearse *Vesti la Giubba, Le Jongleur de Notre Dame,* and *Orpheus* in full makeup and costume in the little theater in his home, located on Twenty-first Street in an unpretentious part of Los Angeles. Hurrell found Novarro to be rather shy, a man whose simple life-style was light-years away from the extravagance exhibited by his film-star contemporaries. He was a religious man, and his bedroom was filled with icons and framed pictures of the saints, as well as a collection of ancient crucifixes from middle Mexico. He was photographed many times over the next few months, at Lafayette Park Place, on Twenty-first Street, and at Poncho's estate in San Marino.

One summer day, Hurrell set up his camera under a giant oak at the Barnes house and caught Novarro dressed in a peasant's tunic, standing next to a white horse. The whole scene was covered with dappled sunlight. When Poncho saw the proofs, she exclaimed: "My God, George, even the horse looks glamorous!"

Norma Shearer

A painful period of trial and error was taking place at Metro-Goldwyn-Mayer: retooling for sound.

With some trepidation, Norma Shearer, the petite, aristocratic wife of pint-sized head of production Irving G. Thalberg, finished *The Trial of Mary Dugan,* her first 100 percent Talking Picture, in which she played a flinty show girl. Since the camera was enclosed in a sound-proof "icebox" that could not be moved, the film was shot straight on, like a stage play. To everyone's relief, Shearer's voice recorded well.

The studio was in the midst of filming *The Hollywood Revue,* a musical in which each M.G.M. top star would do a "turn," when Novarro visited the set. He watched Shearer and John Gilbert rehearse the balcony scene from *Romeo and Juliet,* which was to be photographed in Technicolor. The "gimmick" of the sequence: after the stars had performed the scene in a serious manner, the director yelled "cut" and the players then converted the dialogue into amusing modern-day argot.

At the end of the day, Shearer invited Novarro into her dressing room. Without a word, he handed her a stack of photographs. Spreading the stills on the floor around her chair, she looked in amazement from one print to another. She was enchanted. "Why, Ramon, you've never been photographed like this before!" Then he told her about the unknown photographer with the tiny studio across town.

She smiled mischievously. "He may come in very handy. I have something in mind." She leaned forward and became very earnest. "Irving is preparing a great script called *The Divorcée* that would be perfect for me. This woman is very strong, almost ruthless. She divorces her husband, almost marries someone else, has several flirtations, and finally ends up in Paris with her former husband. The dialogue is very realistic. Oh, I'm so tired of playing show types and brainless ladies. This role has great dramatic range. But Irving won't give *The Divorcée* to me because he thinks I'm *not* alluring! This picture can change my image; afterward, I'll be up for all kinds of new parts. Now, if this man can photograph me like a sexpot. . . ."

On the appointed day a long, cream-colored Rolls-Royce drew up before Hurrell's tiny studio. Shearer emerged, followed by a maid, hairdresser, chauffeur, and a P.R. woman who was not at all impressed with traipsing halfway across Los Angeles for a sitting with an unknown photographer when gifted artists were available in the still gallery at M.G.M. The maid brought in an armload of negligees.

Other than Novarro, this was the first time that Hurrell had come face-to-face with an important movie star. "Welcome to my studio," he said, hiding his nervousness with a laugh, "such as it is!" She surveyed the 15 x 15 room and smiled. "I love your photographs of Mr. Novarro. Now, there is a part in my husband's new picture that I *must* have. Can you turn me into a siren?"

Hurrell grinned. "I'll try."

While she was getting made up and dressed, he energetically arranged lights and camera. He knew very little about Hollywood politics, so movie small talk was out, and at best he was not an expert conversationalist, but he had to break the ice somehow. Classical records had seemed helpful in establishing a mood for Pete. What type of music would interest a potential vamp? Ted Lewis, perhaps? He wound up the Victrola and placed a disk on the turntable. Dressed in a wraparound silver lamé dressing gown, Norma Shearer made her entrance from above to the strains of "When My Baby Smiles At Me."

Singing with the music, Hurrell posed her against a mirror, hoping his apprehension was not apparent. He remembered Steichen's advice: *Never let your subject know when you are baffled. Shoot the film anyway. Make your change on the next shot.*

He struck up two arc lamps, but more illumination was necessary. Because the diaphragm of his old Verito diffusion lens had to be cut to *f*/32 in order to be sharp for reproduction, he removed the screens from the arcs. Film speed was slow; by eliminating the screens, he could use the two- or three-second exposure required to record instant reaction.

He viewed her with the concentrated eye of a painter. "I switched records, then arranged a new neckline for Miss Shearer by pulling the silver material down over one shoulder, exposing as much breast as I could. Then I asked her to reveal her left knee and leg."

"I'm afraid my legs are not my best feature, Mr. Hurrell," she replied in an arch manner, "I never show them."

"They'll be fine . . . stunning from this angle."

But something else was needed. Her hair was the height of 1929 fashion, cut in a medium short bob and marcelled. He asked the hairdresser to recomb the coiffure so that the shaped-to-the-head profile would be softened by down-over-the-forehead bangs. Rather off-key, he sang "Is Everybody Happy?" along with Ted Lewis and exposed plate after plate.

"I found her beautiful from almost any angle," he says. "However, a low light was to be avoided, because this position made her cheeks appear chubby and her chin too full. Her left eye occasionally moved out of focus, but she had such discipline as an actress, that I had no problem."

There were more costume changes, more records, different hairdos, fresh makeups, and toward the end of the sitting Shearer became more relaxed and quite enthusiastic over his exuberance. The cozy atmosphere of the tiny room, intimate and warm, abetted by the jazz recordings, was providing the right mood for sultry poses. Several times, the Victrola ran down with hilarious results: Ted Lewis, always slow with a lyric, became impossibly languid. She was much amused. Shearer, accustomed to the cold, damp, sterile surroundings of the still gallery, was *having a good time.*

Hurrell was in the darkroom as soon as the entourage had left, developing the sixty-odd plates in a tray. The negs were very special . . . she looked like a sophisticated woman of the world, waiting for an invitation. He could not stem his enthusiasm. He danced from table to chair to fireplace to stair, securing the films with pushpins until the studio resembled a drying room of a laundry. Then, singing at the top of his lungs, Hurrell went out to celebrate.

The next day, he sent a stack of 8 x 10 red proofs to the studio, and waited by the telephone. "I had a feeling that my whole career depended upon the Shearer photographs," Hurrell says, "And, as it turned out, I was right. Finally word came that she had gone yachting and the proofs had faded in the sunshine. Would I kindly send along an additional selection? There was also another question—how had Miss Shearer acquired 'klieg eyes'? She had been in misery for two days." Hurrell had not known that the brilliant, flickering arc lamps must not be used without screens!

Norma Shearer triumphantly showed the proofs to her husband. Even without retouching, she looked sensational. Thalberg looked at the

Norma Shearer, first sitting. 1929.

8

shots. There before him was *The Divorcée*—alluring, mysterious, a thinly veiled promise in her eyes, a "come hither" look to her mouth. "All right, Norma," he laughed, "you've convinced me. And, by the way, since our temperamental Ruth Harriet Louise has left, I think we can use this man Hurrell in our still gallery."

Howard Strickling, who worked for Pete Smith in the publicity department at the studio, telephoned Hurrell with the good news. "There is just one thing: we need you *now*. Oh, by the way, the pay is a hundred and fifty dollars for a five-day week. Of course, there will be more money if things work out."

Hurrell was delighted. Considering the studio executives had only seen the Shearer photographs, which from their point of view might have been a fluke, the offer was generous. Besides, his own finances were in more jeopardy than usual. With Wall Street in a panic and 60 percent of Americans taking home less than $2,000 per year, the job at M.G.M. seemed heaven-sent.

He could not know that he was on the brink of a career that would eclipse many of the achievements of the very stars he would photograph. Nor did he dream that almost fifty years later, he would still be working in Hollywood. In the future were the sobriquets by which he would become famous: "The Ziegfeld of the Camera"—"The Magic Man of Hollywood"—"The Madcap of the Still Camera"—"The Glamour Boy of the Lens"—"The Horatio Alger of Photography"—"The Rembrandt of the Shutters."

M.G.M.

Hurrell turned his La Salle Roadster smoothly into the parking lot across from the main gate at M.G.M. on Washington Boulevard in Culver City, picked up his pass, and was given directions on how to locate Howard Strickling's office.

This was his first time on a motion-picture lot, and Hurrell was amazed at the ordered disorder; clumps of extras in Spanish costumes stood about chatting animatedly; boys on bicycles peddled to and fro down the main thoroughfares; an occasional chauffeured limousine drove by, occupants sheltered by curtains. Men in business suits and workmen in overalls were everywhere. M.G.M. was a miniature city with huge buildings the size of airplane hangars, whose mammoth doors, open to the winds, looked like giant gaping mouths. Hurrell was struck with a sense of mystery and fantasy and romance. How was he going to fit into this strange and provocative make-believe metropolis?

"Strick" greeted him warmly—the beginning of a lifelong friendship—and took him next door to meet publicity head Pete Smith, a thin, humorous, bespectacled man, whose desk was piled high with press releases and stacks of photographs. Strick then took Hurrell on a whirlwind tour of the lot, which seemed to grow in size as they walked from one department and sound stage to another.

Hurrell learned about the beginnings of the studio, which like everything else connected with the motion-picture industry, was part business and part speculation. It had all started in 1915 with a land promoter named Harry Culver, who was loaded down with acreage that no one wanted, located some eight miles from the beach at Venice. From headquarters in the eight-story Culver Hotel, the only building within sight, Culver dreamed of the day when Washington Boulevard would be dotted with exclusive shops and the area given over to stately mansions with wide, spacious lawns. His great problem was how to interest business people in this flat, somewhat arid terrain. Then he hit upon a plan. If he could sell some of the land to a motion-picture studio, hundreds, perhaps thousands, of employees would settle in the area, an invasion that could become the nucleus of a thriving community. If Harry Culver was a dreamer, the producers queried about his scheme were not. What person in his right mind would build a studio so far away from Hollywood? But when scrappy little "Uncle Carl" Laemmle took over 203 acres near Cahuenga Pass, where the hills dropped into San Fernando Valley, Culver's hopes rose anew. He offered to *give away* land to an enterprising producer—but there were still no takers.

Then Thomas H. Ince, whose small studio near the beach and Sunset Boulevard was troubled by fog, took Harry Culver up on his offer and demanded sixteen acres fronting Washington Boulevard. He built five glass-enclosed stages and several office buildings. But Ince was troubled with financial problems and became (as Bosley Crowther explained in his history of M.G.M., *The Lion's Share*) one of the elements in Triangle Film Company, which moved into the studio. Triangle did not do well either, beset as it was with conditions brought about by World War I, executive clashes, and tight money. So Samuel Goldwyn entered the fray and assumed control of the now abandoned lot. Through various manipulations, in May 1924, Loew's Inc. (which had acquired Metro Pictures Corp. in 1920) organized Metro-Goldwyn-Mayer Pictures Corp. through a merger with Metro and Goldwyn, with the participation of Louis B. Mayer—although Goldwyn himself, through a twist of fate, had left his own company in 1922.

M.G.M. was then a comparatively new studio, with the modern sound stages that Hurrell faced on his tour with Strick that first day. He was awed by the filming ritual. The large sets looked minuscule stuck away in the corner of the stages, overstrung with catwalks, hung with lights of various sizes and wattages, all surrounded by massive camera equipment and attended by what seemed like hundreds of technicians, each with a separate job to perform. The floors were piled with hundreds of miles of cable, or "spaghetti." Red lights flashed, signaling the beginning of scenes; bells rang; cries of "Camera!" "Action!" "Cut and print!" sliced the air.

Yes, Hurrell was told, *The Divorcée* was shooting, but Miss Shearer, who had become pregnant, was at home. . . . Yes, Miss Garbo was working, but her set, as always, was closed. . . . Yes, Mr. Novarro was on the lot, but was recording "Redi Pagliacci" for his new film, *Call of the Flesh*. . . . Yes, Miss Crawford's set, *Our Blushing Brides*, was open. They stood on the sidelines and watched the star rehearse a dance number.

Then Strick whisked Hurrell away to the place that would become his home for the next three years. The still gallery, a completely self-contained unit, was built on a roof, three stories up from the busy central thoroughfare. He was introduced to Al St. Hilaire, who had started with the old Metro Company and had been Ruth Harriet Louise's assistant, and to retoucher Andrew Korf, who worked in a cubbyhole near the adjacent laboratory.

The room, Hurrell saw at a glance, was not as large as he had imagined, but was still big enough to hold a battery of equipment as well as a makeup table surrounded by a large screen, behind which the players could change clothing. The roof was made of glass panes, under which was strung a tarpaulin that moved back and forth on pulleys to admit or restrict light. A door opened out on the roof, a refuge to be used by the trio of men while a female star was dressing. It was a comfortable setup.

Hurrell became familiar with the equipment. Besides the "monster" 8 x 10 portrait camera, he had the use of various sizes of lamps, each with its own name: 500-watt spotlights were called *babies;* 1,000-watt, *juniors;* 2,000-watt, *seniors;* and 5,000-watts with scrims (used for "fill light" after other lamps were placed in position around the subject) were referred to as *broads.*

Hurrell quickly entered into the still-gallery routine. Publicity always booked sittings at least a day in advance, so he always knew whom he was scheduled to shoot. A larger laboratory on another part of the lot catered to the needs of the still photographers who worked on the sets. That operation, headed by Clarence Sinclair Bull, was run quite apart from Hurrell's portrait department, overseen wholly by Pete Smith and Howard Strickling.

One thing was missing in the gallery—music. On his way to lunch, Hurrell stopped Strick: "I've always worked with a phonograph. Do you think you could find me one on the lot?"

That afternoon, a new Victrola was brought up to the still gallery and placed in the corner. Passers-by never knew what kind of music would be floating out over the rooftops. A little starlet might respond to "The Afternoon of a Faun," while a top dramatic personality might relate better to "Tiger Rag," but when Hurrell was in high form, working at breakneck speed, the music was always jazz, jazz, jazz.

Lon Chaney

The first important male star on the lot scheduled for a Hurrell sitting was not the romantic John Gilbert, the handsome Nils Asther, or the dashing Rod La Rocque, but chief bogeyman, Lon Chaney. His reputation as a portrayer of grotesque characters had even earned him a song parody in *The Hollywood Revue*, performed by Gus Edwards: "Lon Chaney Will Get You If You Don't Watch Out."

Chaney had a late call for *The Unholy Three*, and showed up in full

makeup. He wore a pin-striped suit, a bowler hat, and carried a ventrilo-
quist dummy in his arms. Chaney, forty-seven, looked at least ten years
older. "Don't worry about the wrinkles, they're my trademark," he
laughed, "just go ahead and shoot 'em." He sat down, placed the dummy
on his knee, and immediately assumed the character of Echo in the film,
menacing, sinister, and evil.

Hurrell was impressed with this metamorphosis, an instantaneous
change from the affable man who had entered the gallery a moment
before. The actor's presence was almost overpowering, and Hurrell
quickly rolled a lamp into place at a low angle, so that a foreboding
shadow was cast on the background wall. He was to use this shadow technique throughout his career.

Chaney was involved in an odd cycle. He was then the only "character star" on the lot whose films made millions of dollars. (Later Marie
Dressler and Wallace Beery would achieve immense popularity and box
office in older roles.) Chaney specialized in parts that no one else could, or
would, touch, and his legion of fans thronged theaters at the advent of
each new picture to see what new horror makeup he had devised. His
gallery of characterizations included the blind pirate, Pew, in *Treasure
Island;* the mad, crippled crook in *Flesh and Blood;* the deranged scientist in
While Paris Sleeps. But his chefs d'oeuvres were the hunchback Quasimodo
in *The Hunchback of Notre Dame* and the title role in *The Phantom of the
Opera.* Each of these monsters, deformed in face or body or both, nevertheless was portrayed as a human being, and as they suffered the indigni-
ties of mankind, audiences everywhere sorrowed along with them.

With each new property, Chaney spent weeks designing not only
facial makeup, but a special walk and separate set of gestures befitting the
character. He sometimes used torturing devices that turned him into a variety of cripples. He had lost his teeth years before, and different sorts of
dentures were employed—or not employed, as in *Mr. Wu.* He was the
last major star on the lot to make the transition from silents to talkies
other than Greta Garbo, who would shortly film *Anna Christie.*

Just as he was known as "The Man With a Thousand Faces," so did
he intend to become "The Man With a Thousand Voices." He was most
conscious of sound because both his mother and father had been born
deaf. He attributed his art of mimicry to the fact that he had learned not
only facial expression, but also body language while communicating with
them. In 1930 he signed a new five-year contract with the studio and
planned to remake many of his silent films as talkies. In *The Unholy Three,*
he unveiled five different voices, as the main character Echo (Echo, strong
man Hercules and a cigar-smoking midget who played a baby were the
bizarre trio), the dummy, an old woman, a young girl, and a parrot.

During the shooting, Hurrell noticed that Chaney treated the
dummy as an individual, not as a prop. When he wanted some shots of
the star alone, he gently removed the dummy from Chaney's knee.

"Now, how about some straight stuff?" Hurrell asked.

Chaney's malevolent expression changed. He became affable again and laughed out loud. "Not today. I don't feel comfortable being photographed as myself." He got up, shook Hurrell's hand with a sort of finality, and tenderly picked up the dummy. At the door he paused and turned. "Good-bye," he said, plaintively, and disappeared down the stairs.

A few months later, when word spread over the lot that Chaney had died of throat cancer, that final "good-bye" haunted Hurrell.

Lon Chaney as Echo in the talkie version of The Unholy Three. *1930.*

Greta Garbo

"Garbo greeted me with a merry 'Alloo M'ster 'urell!'" Hurrell reminisces. "Her hair was straw colored, eyes pale blue, and her complexion a joy, unblemished and fresh. She wore very little makeup and her eyes were fringed with the longest natural lashes I had ever seen. She was in a good mood. *Romance*, in which she played Cavallini, a notorious opera star, had finished filming. In fact, I had photographed her leading man, Lewis Stone, only a few days before. She brought along three costume changes, old-fashioned gowns with Watteau hats, none of which were very interesting or photogenic. I would have much preferred to bring my camera on the set and shoot her among the fancy props for the picture instead of taking dress shots in the gallery, but that was not allowed.

"By the time I had taken a meter reading and focused the lens, Garbo had turned sober. I was not pleased with the flat light. Making a quick

THROUGH PAGE *19:*
Greta Garbo as Cavallini, the opera star in Romance. *1930.*

decision, I reached up and pulled the ropes that controlled the tarpaulin on the ceiling and bright sunlight flooded into the room. I posed her full length against a plain wall that showed off her costume of dark velvet and ermine as well as the Princess Eugenie hat, but I still wished I had some decorative paraphernalia to set the scene. I hummed and jumped up and down and the result was a slight smile, which I caught. Thereafter, she was pensive; she did not appear to respond very much to my popular recordings.

"While Al St. Hilaire prepared additional plates for the camera, I asked her to change to a more interesting gown that had a plunging, heart-shaped neckline, partially obscured by a heavy chinchilla wrap. I had to work with the bulky costumes as best I could. I turned her this way and that, and found that she was beautiful from any angle. I'm sure I could have photographed the back of her head with interesting results.

"She was pleasantly amused by my antics, which now grew more and more ridiculous as I tried to penetrate that marvelous composure and throw her off guard. But I felt I was getting very little reaction. Finally, I almost fell over some cables and she laughed out loud. The camera bulb was still in my hand, and in the split second while I regained balance, I instinctively squeezed the bulb. The result was a rare shot that many photographers had tried to catch—and failed—a gay, laughing Garbo— exactly the way I found her to be in person."

Garbo finally laughed. 1930.

After she left, Hurrell looked over his lighting equipment. He needed a small lamp that could be moved dexterously back and forth to achieve special effects. The babies, juniors, seniors, and broads all had a purpose, but could not be maneuvered with ease. He had noticed, while visiting an occasional set, that the microphone was suspended from a long boom, or pole, placed over the head of a performer, just out of camera range. He went to Strick: "I want a small light that can be suspended from a boom. Is there such a thing?"

"No," the publicity man countered impatiently, "it would have to be built. It would cost a fortune. I'm afraid you've struck out this time. What's wrong with the equipment in the gallery?"

"Nothing. But I've got to work my head off to get results. When I'm trying to get expression out of my subjects, I can't be worried about the damned lamps." Hurrell was becoming heated. "With all the other lights set, I could adjust this 'boom light' in a twinkling. Now, do I get it, or not?"

Strick sighed. "I suppose so, but I'll have to bury the cost somewhere. . . ."

When portraits where Hurrell had employed the new boom light began to appear, cinematographers all over the lot became curious. How had this new guy achieved these startling effects? Singly, on one pretext or another, the cameramen made the trek up the stairs to the still gallery.

Six months later, every sound stage featured a boom light as part of the equipment repertoire.

John Gilbert

During the last part of the silent era, M.G.M.'s box-office king was screen lover John Gilbert, whose string of leading ladies included Renee Adoree, Joan Crawford, Jeanne Eagels, and Mae Murray. In films like *Flesh and the Devil* and *Love*, both with Greta Garbo, he drew genuine sparks on celluloid. He spoke with his eyes and he was a master of pantomime. His enormous female fan following loved his swagger, dash, and elegance, his true sense of drama. He also had a widely publicized romance with Garbo. But, with the addition of words on a sound track, Gilbert's smoldering passion appeared grotesque.

The New York Times pinpointed his problem in its review of *His Glorious Night*, October 5, 1929: ". . . It is quite evident that the producers intend to keep Mr. Gilbert, even now that he talks in his amorous scenes, before the public as the great screen lover, for in this current narrative, this actor constantly repeats 'I love you' to the Princess Orsolini as he kisses her. In fact, his many protestations of affection while embracing this charming girl . . . caused a large female contingent in the theatre yesterday afternoon to giggle and laugh."

It was not his voice that was truly at fault (the *Times* reported: "His voice is pleasant, but one not rich in nuances."), but the selection of screen material. His second talking film, *Redemption*, started before and finished after *His Glorious Night*, was not popular, and when Hurrell came to the lot, Gilbert was being cast against type as a rough seaman in *Way for a Sailor*.

Gilbert, then, was not in the best psychological mood when his appointment came up for a photographic session. Hurrell relates: "He was thirty-three years old and beginning to show his age, yet he was an excellent subject, easily photographed from most angles. Being uncomfortable before the microphone and more than ever conscious of the camera, he was ill at ease. Al St. Hilaire placed a classical recording on the Victrola and Gilbert loosened up. He had been fond of music being played on the set during his silent love scenes, and the stark silence of a sound set bothered him."

Hurrell, as always, worked quickly. "I knew that I couldn't keep him for very long. He fidgeted and perspired, and even when I played an upbeat tango, and danced around the studio, I could not promote a laugh. Finally he got up from his chair and said, 'That's enough. I've got to go now!' He slipped quietly down the stairs." It was many months before Strick could coax him back to the gallery and by then the star was truly on the decline.

John Gilbert, near the end of his career, would not smile for Hurrell's still camera. 1931.

Norma Shearer

After Irving, Jr., was born, the Thalbergs moved to a beach house in Santa Monica. Shearer came back to the studio to play the reckless, sophisticated daughter of a famous alcoholic attorney (Lionel Barrymore) in *A Free Soul*. Shearer's new contract, stipulating $6,000 a week, was one of the highest sums paid in Hollywood and cemented her position, if any reinforcement was necessary, as Queen of the Lot.

Fresh from seeing the "rushes" on the picture, she came into Hurrell's gallery alone, with only a couple of costume changes thrown casually over her arm. A scant year had passed since her first sitting at Lafayette Park Place, but there were subtle differences in attitude displayed by both star and photographer. They laughed, easy with each other now.

Hurrell, St. Hilaire, and Korf withdrew to the rooftop while she changed clothing. She appeared in a daring, silver-sequin, off-the-shoulder gown, held up by sequin straps. For a moment she held her aristocratic pose, then shifted her body and became, in an instant, a "free soul." Swaying with the music, she assumed a slumbrous pose: she knew what was expected of her. Hurrell didn't need to coax an unwilling smile from her lips or rearrange her garments.

In the middle of the sitting, she looked up and frowned. "You know, George, it seems so strange to be up here, when we've got those magnificent sets down on the stage. I would feel much more at home being photographed there. I think my clothes would look better, too."

"But Miss Shearer," Hurrell protested, "there is a good still man on the picture. You know I can't shoot on the sets."

"I know. I know. But I don't see why you can't come down *after* the cast leaves. Let me speak to Irving."

He shot more closeups, one of which would be used for advertising art, and then she left for the day.

It took time to break precedent at the studio but finally, just before *A Free Soul* was finished, Shearer received permission for Hurrell to come to the set. It was an extremely expensive procedure, since the film crew was required to stand by while the still shots were being made. Because the heavy jumbo portrait camera could not be brought down from the gallery, Hurrell and St. Hilaire reported to the camera department and checked out a portable view camera, a three-legged tripod, "holders" that were already loaded with film, and various lighting equipment. Because Stage 22 was a block and a half away, a limousine transported them to the set, where they were joined by three other limousines: the first with Shearer alone, the second with a makeup man and a hairdresser, and the third with a maid and wardrobe girl with numerous costume changes. The jaded film crew, schooled to be blasé about all happenings, looked in amazement as the star and her entourage were helped from the Cadillacs.

"The photographs," Hurrell says, "were splendid. Shearer was right. The costumes did look better, and surrounded by the actual sets, character was more easily established. Psychologically, it all worked. After that, I shot on the sets as often as permitted. No longer was I plagued with a plain backdrop or lack of props to work with." Taking portraits on the set then became his specialty during all the glory years ahead.

Later, when Shearer was filming *Strange Interlude*, with Clark Gable, she thought one of the living room sets was especially lovely and told Strick that she wanted photographs taken there. The next morning, Shearer and her following arrived as the set was being reassembled

Irving Thalberg.

Norma Shearer poses on a film set for publicity pictures, although no film was in progress. 1934.

Norma Shearer. 1936.

Norma Shearer as Elizabeth Barrett Browning in The Barretts of Wimpole Street. *1934.*

especially for her. "It won't be ready for an hour," she was told. Conscience-stricken, and thinking about the expense, she telephoned Strick: "Oh, you should have told me the set had already been struck! I had no idea. . . ."

"But she was the Queen," Hurrell explains, "and what she wanted, she usually got; no expense was ever spared."

In the 1930–31 period, Shearer was nominated for an Academy Award for both *The Divorcée* and a film released earlier in the year, *Their Own Desire.* When she won the golden statuette for *The Divorcée,* two people figuratively shared that exquisite moment of triumph—George Hurrell, whose daring photographs had convinced Thalberg she could do the role, and Thalberg himself.

FAR LEFT: *Marie Dressler as dowager Carlotta Vance in* Dinner at Eight. *1933.*

LEFT: *As Min in* Min and Bill. *1930.*

Marie Dressler

Rotund, homely, sixtyish, character actress Marie Dressler was the studio's all-around favorite personality. She had won favor as a rowdy, slapstick comedienne as early as 1914 with her film version of *Tillie's Punctured Romance*, with Charles Chaplin and Mabel Normand. Her rambunctious comic roles continued until her career lost momentum in the twenties, but then her star rose anew with the advent of "talkies." Her stage-trained voice was exactly as audiences had imagined: deeply resonant and as perfect for her as were her dewlap and girth. She made seven pictures in 1930, all hits.

A wave of lavender perfume preceded her entrance into the gallery. "I've got a whole day," she announced in seriocomic tones. "Now let's do something interesting."

"Her face was the most expressive I had shot up to that time," Hurrell recalls. "She reacted instantly to my moods. I didn't have to worry about making her look slim. She slapped her well-corseted derriere. 'That's all me!' she laughed. 'I want some smiling photos, because your shots of me as that old drunken windbag Marthe in *Anna Christie* ain't me. I don't want the public to forget I'm a comedienne.'"

And they didn't—one foray into serious drama could not erase a lifetime as a comic. The Dressler line most often remembered by film buffs occurred later, in the hilarious screen adaptation of the Kaufman-Ferber success *Dinner at Eight*. In the film, Jean Harlow, as a rather loose lady, attracts the attention of Dressler, the brusque dowager. "Do you know," comments Harlow offhandedly, "that guy said machinery is going to take the place of every profession."

At her home. 1934.

"Oh my dear," replies the grand old dame, "that's something *you* need never worry about!"

Hurrell's own favorite shot of Marie, he says, "was taken in the corner of her living room, as she sat in her favorite chair, crocheting—just like my grandmother."

When St. Hilaire developed the films of Dressler, he delivered the collection of 8 x 10 negatives to Andrew Korf's retouching table. "You're going to have fun with these, but George says not to take away *too* much!"

Korf began his delicate job by turning over a negative, emulsion side up, and dabbing a bit of retouching fluid on the "balloon tires" under Dressler's eyes, carefully feathering the "dope" into the surrounding area with a small piece of cotton. This procedure eliminated blotching and streaking. He then selected the softest architect's lead—HB—which he fitted into a metal holder and sandpapered until the point was rapier sharp. Since the light portions of the negative turned up as dark areas in the finished contact print, he peered though a five-inch magnifying glass that he swung over the negative, and with sure, deft strokes filled up the lower lid area to the proper value of the surrounding skin texture. Using the same technique, he would later completely eliminate Joan Crawford's famous off-screen freckles.

Wallace Beery

Like Lon Chaney, Wallace Beery at forty-five was proud of the lines in his face. "I'm not the glamour-puss type," he would laugh. Yet Hurrell discovered, ironically, that, like Garbo, he had a photographically perfect face that could be shot from any direction. Some players could be photographed only from certain angles, because they appeared totally different when photographed from other angles. But Beery looked like Beery from any angle.

Mayer and Thalberg brought him to M.G.M. for the role of the condemned convict in *The Big House*, which was shooting when Hurrell came to the studio. The actor had appeared in forty-five feature films, plus a great many one-reel comedies. He was an alumnus of the Ringling Circus and musical shows in New York, and had written, directed, and produced short films very early in his career. Beery had also married and divorced Gloria Swanson in the late teens. During the next few years, he was to become one of the most beloved character men in Hollywood, and in 1931–32 would be presented with an Academy Award for *The Champ*, sharing the dual award with Fredric March for *Dr. Jekyll and Mr. Hyde*.

To catch the proper atmosphere of bleak prison life, Hurrell was summoned to the set of *The Big House*, and took memorable character studies that would have been impossible in the gallery. Later he brought his camera over to Mines Field and shot photographs of Beery and his new plane, which Beery flew back and forth between Los Angeles and his cabin at Mammoth Lakes.

Bert Lahr

Bert Lahr, who would gain world renown as the Cowardly Lion in *The Wizard of Oz*, filmed at M.G.M. in 1939, actually made his film debut at the studio eight years earlier. He re-created his role of Rusty Krause opposite Charlotte Greenwood's Pansy Botts in the George White musical comedy, *Flying High*, the title of which referred to a long aerocopter sequence involving the incongruous couple.

Hurrell went to the set to photograph a line of chorus girls in bathing suits—other than a few leg shots, his first experience with cheesecake. He posed the girls sitting on a piano, with Lahr on the bench, contemplating five pairs of legs. After the chorines left, Lahr looked up with a wicked gleam in his eye, "Want some mug shots?" he asked, then went into a wicked burlesque routine that had Hurrell in stitches.

He never did get the mug shots.

Jimmy Durante

Jimmy Durante popped his head in the gallery doorway, grinned maniacally at Hurrell, and shouted: "So yur de guy who's giving me competish! Some wise guy on da set said I gotta meetcha. Said I shud come up here and take a few lessons. Said ya got da best comedy schtick in town!"

Hurrell laughed, "I'm flattered. What kind of music do you like, Mr. Durante?"

"Call me Jimmy. Anything—as long as it's Broadway."

In a moment, Eddie Cantor singing "Whoopee " sailed out of the phonograph and Durante jumped up and down. "Let's get this show on da road, 'cause I'm rarin' ta go!"

"Sit down, Jimmy, I'm ready." Hurrell started to sing along with Cantor, " 'Another bride, another groom. . . .' " As Durante reacted, he squeezed the bulb. " 'Another happy honeymoon. . . .' " He squeezed the bulb again. " 'And that's the reason, it's the season, for making. . . .' "

"Whoopee!" Durante screamed, and Hurrell got another shot.

"Jimmy, turn to your right. See that statue?"

Durante swung around and confronted a small, nude, abstract figure, "Yeah, she's gorgeous!"

As he said "gorgeous," Hurrell squeezed the bulb. "Jimmy, that's great." He took one last shot.

"Hey, when we gonna shoot de pitchers?" Durante asked, suddenly sober.

"We already have. It's a wrap."

"What?"

"It's a wrap. Five o'clock. Time to go home."

Durante made for the door, scratching his head. He turned at the threshold and looked back and laughed. "I shoulda knowed I'd be had!"

OVERLEAF LEFT: *Wallace Beery in* The Big House, *1930; as Pancho Villa in* Viva Villa!, *1934; and with his plane at Mines Field, 1930.*

RIGHT TOP: *Bert Lahr as Rusty Krause in* Flying High. *1931.*

BOTTOM: *Jimmy Durante. 1931.*

*Robert Montgomery in the
portrait gallery. 1932.*

*Robert Montgomery with the
ponies at the Polo Field near
Will Rogers's home. 1931.*

Robert Montgomery

Robert Montgomery, whom Hurrell had photographed for the first time on the *Big House* set, was called upon to do a number of pictures in support of the big female stars. Pencil thin and somewhat fragile looking in person, he photographed in a more attractive and robust way. And, although he had good roles in films, like *Untamed* with Crawford, *Their Own Desire* with Shearer, and *Inspiration* with Garbo (in which he was mainly used for "window dressing"), he was at his best when cast as a light comedian.

He was rather cold and uncommunicative on the lot, but he was also overworked, having made eight pictures in 1930 alone. In the gallery, he reacted very little to Hurrell's shenanigans and appeared indifferent to music of any kind. He remained stoic even when a wild foxtrot blared forth from the phonograph. Still, Hurrell was able to take interesting shots by paying more attention to the lighting than to Montgomery's expression. Although unsmiling and bored, a sly, whimsical quality often came through.

Elected president of the Screen Actor's Guild in 1935, he was to have a highly unusual off-screen career. After making fifty-eight films, he enjoyed several vocations—television producer, TV consultant for President Eisenhower, and a director of Macy's department store in New York.

None of these very special qualities that would later enable him to be so versatile was apparent during the early days. But Montgomery was a proud father, and when daughter Elizabeth (destined to become an actress in her own right) was born, Hurrell took his camera over to the house off Benedict Canyon to photograph the baby in the crib. Later he shot Montgomery among the horses at the Polo Field, where Will Rogers, Darryl Zanuck and the Hollywood boys played every Sunday.

Twenty years later, when he was producing "Robert Montgomery Presents" for television, Hurrell telephoned on one pretext or another and found him still the frosty, aloof man whom he remembered so well.

Leslie Howard

"Howard was the typical Englishman in front of the lens," says Hurrell, "formal and rather reserved. Yet he could be loose-jointed, too, and joke in a kind of dry way. 'Let's *do* get on with it, Mr. Hurrell,' he would say, changing his coat and tie for the next shot. He made three pictures at the studio, the best probably *A Free Soul* with Shearer and *Five and Ten* with Davies, but he didn't limber up until he made comedies like *Stand-In* over at Warner Bros. He had a kind of melancholia in his eyes that photographed very well, and he had a haunting quality. No one ever said, 'Hi, Les'—he was 'Mr. Howard' on the lot."

Robert Young

Robert Young was twenty-four years old when he signed a contract with the studio. His first film on the lot was *The Sin of Madelon Claudet*, in which he played the son whom Helen Hayes sends to medical school by prostituting herself. It was a good role and when she won an Academy Award, his stock rose. He went on to play a variety of leading "son" roles, both at M.G.M. and on loan to other companies.

Hurrell says, "I used few tricks with Bob. He was always relaxed in front of the camera, but I found his face in repose much more interesting than when animated, so I did not often shoot him laughing. He had a warm but unprepossessing personality, not the drive of a Gable or the ambition of a Montgomery. I photographed him several times during the next decade, and in the late sixties when he played *Marcus Welby, M.D.*, on television, we had quite a reunion. He was still the relaxed and unpretentious man that I had recalled so fondly. The forty years in between had done well by him. Of course, his face was lined and his hair was gray—but then, alas, so were mine!"

Robert Young. 1931.

Helen Hayes

Studios all over town were still raiding Broadway for nonaccented players whose voices were already "placed," and who also could remember dialogue with some alacrity. Up for consideration was thirty-one-year-old Helen Hayes, who was making a reputation for herself, especially in the great James M. Barrie hit, *What Every Woman Knows* (which she pressed into service again some twenty-eight years later for an extended Broadway run and a national tour). Hayes, though not exactly born in a trunk, had made her stage debut at the age of eight as one of the title waifs in *Babes In The Woods*. She was summoned to M.G.M. by Edgar Selwyn, who was to direct a picture first called *Lullaby*, and then *The Sin of Madelon Claudet*, which was rewritten on a day-by-day basis by her husband, playwright Charles MacArthur.

Hurrell had heard that Mrs. MacArthur was difficult to photograph, and when she came into the gallery, he found her very attractive but quite nervous.

"I always have butterflies before going on stage," she said plaintively, "and I feel the same way now."

Helen Hayes on the set of The Sin of Madelon Claudet. *1931.*

He seated her comfortably in a chair and picked out a recording of "You Will Remember Vienna," which St. Hilaire placed on the Victrola. She relaxed as the music took over. Hurrell saw that a straight front pose was best. As she relaxed with the waltz, he caught a rather whimsical, far-away look in her eyes. She reacted as he sang along with the recording, making up his own words as he went along. He exposed so many plates, one after the other, that St. Hilaire complained that he could not keep the holders loaded quickly enough. But Hurrell knew that he had to keep shooting before *he* began to get butterflies in his stomach.

Helen Hayes, who thought she was not beautiful, was enchanted with the photographs, which showed her young and lovely. Hayes won an Academy Award for her film debut, and ten years later in New York was still telling Hurrell about her butterflies.

Alfred Lunt & Lynn Fontanne

That magic Broadway couple, Alfred Lunt and Lynn Fontanne, had been coaxed west by Thalberg to make a film version of their highly successful stage piece, Ferenc Molnar's *The Guardsman*, performed in 1924, to be directed by old pro Sidney Franklin. Thalberg had just finished shooting *Private Lives*, with Norma Shearer and Robert Montgomery and, more than any director on the lot, he was familiar with ultra-sophisticated stage-to-screen properties. He found the Lunts cooperative but tense and somewhat in awe of the sound camera.

While *The Guardsman* was in preproduction, Strick booked the pair for portraits, and they arrived in street clothes, a bit breathless from the three-story climb. St. Hilaire had just placed a recording of Gloria Swanson singing "Love, Your Magic Spell Is Everywhere" on the Victrola. "Nice touch," Lunt said graciously, "nice touch." His wife merely looked bewildered.

Hurrell selected a more upbeat tune to which they reacted not at all, but the music helped build up *his* own shooting tempo. They assumed a pose and he performed a bit of a soft-shoe routine. When he waved his arms wildly they appeared to be very nonplussed. Their marvelous composure was held throughout the sitting. Hurrell was very careful about the lighting. Because of their ages (Fontanne was forty-four and Lunt thirty-seven), he would have preferred shooting them in some of the romantic and flattering costumes from the picture, which was to be stunningly designed, but these portraits were needed for advance publicity.

Alfred Lunt and Lynn Fontanne before the start of The Guardsman. *1931.*

He discovered that Fontanne's old-world type of patrician beauty was shown to better advantage straight on; side views were to be avoided because her face appeared too full. Lunt was much more photogenic. Hurrell thanked God—and Strick—for the boom light, which he angled into place from the right, casting an interesting shadow on the left side of the actor's face.

Strick encountered Hurrell as he was checking off the lot that afternoon. "My God, George," he said, "what did you do to the Lunts?"

"What do you mean? Nothing! Why?"

"They've been photographed a hell of a lot and they know these pics are going to be the absolute nadir!"

The proofs were sent to the Lunts in San Francisco, where they were enjoying a brief holiday before starting the picture. A few days later, Strick sidled up to Hurrell in the commissary and put his arm around him. He was all smiles. "Alfred Lunt just called from up north," he exclaimed, "and do you know what? He ordered all kinds of prints. Best photos they've ever had taken!"

Before the famed duo left the lot, however, there occurred one of the titillating episodes in the history of the studio. Word spread that Miss Fontanne, realistic to the core, had performed a crucial bathtub scene without benefit of the usual upper covering worn in such circumstances. This would not have been recorded on film, since the water was at a decent level, except that during the shooting of the scene, she was surprised by a sound and inappropriately half raised up out of the tub. The resulting footage was long treasured.

The finished prints of the Hurrell session showed Lunt and Fontanne in deceptively casual poses—shots that might have been taken for the pages of *Town and Country,* rather than *Photoplay* magazine.

Hedda Hopper

Hedda Hopper, née Elda Furry, had just celebrated her forty-sixth birthday when she posed for Hurrell in 1931. However, she had hidden her birth year so successfully for so long that she probably did not know how old she really was. Even as an actress, Hopper had always been a celebrity watcher. Her curiosity about the private lives of her fellow actors would eventually hold her in good stead: in 1937 she turned out her first Hollywood column. But even with her duties as a public gossip, until the day she died at the age of eighty-one, she always thought of herself as an actress. Indeed, she appeared in some eighty pictures, the last being *The Oscar*, released a month after her death.

"Hedda Hopper," Hurrell recalls, "was gay, sophisticated, and incredibly stylish—both in dress and in manner. Perhaps her greatest quality was that she liked people. She didn't automatically rate you on a scale from one to ten. She was witty and fun, and some of her mischievous spirit always came through in her photographs. Handsome rather than beautiful, she had portrayed so many world-weary society gals in pictures that she knew her public didn't expect her to look like an ingenue. She was always amused at my madcap manner. We remained friends throughout her lifetime, and she would sometimes call me and say: 'My God, George, help me out. Got any dirt? I've got to get this damned column out every day—and it ain't easy!' "

Hedda Hopper. 1931.

Jackie Cooper. 1931.

Jackie Cooper

"In the old days, posing child stars for the still camera was a pain in the neck," Hurrell recalls. "They performed much better for the motion-picture camera, because of being involved in action. Static sittings were pure agony for both the kids and the photographer. And there was always the mother or the guardian outside of camera range, threatening or cajoling her charge while you were trying to establish a mood. It is much better now, with 35 mm, because we work so quickly that the children don't have time to become bored, to fidget because of an uncomfortable chair, or to perspire because of the hot lights.

"To avoid these and similar problems, I always tried to take my camera to the sets. The kids were much more relaxed and at home, and since I worked very fast, I always got some interesting stuff.

"Jackie Cooper first came to M.G.M. in 1931 for *The Champ* with Wallace Beery. In that film he performed his famous crying scene at the death of the old prizefighter. The picture was difficult to make because Beery did not like to work with child actors—especially an appealing and winsome talent like Jackie. But I found Jackie easy to pose. The trick was *not* to pose him, actually. He would laugh at my clowning and pout when I looked sad. The best pictures I ever shot of him were with a dog, because there is always a special vein of feeling between a child and a pet. But animals can be a problem, too, because they are usually much more photogenic than the person with whom they are photographed. Jackie survived as an actor, director, and producer. The fact that he's still working today shows the great determination he displayed even as a boy."

40

Jean Harlow

"I genuinely liked Jean Harlow," Hurrell remembers, "we were on the same wavelength from the beginning. I had a job to do and she had a job to do: I was there to make her as beautiful as possible, and she had the necessary sex appeal. Although ambitious and determined to become a star, she was also casual and fun loving, with no pretense whatsoever, and with a natural wit and a humorous attitude about the whole studio system. She was spirited and loved having a good time; in fact, she held the unofficial dice record at Agua Caliente Casino in Mexico, with thirty-four straight passes. She was never taken in by anyone, except perhaps her mother and stepfather, who were predatory types. When she was with them, she was quieter and more aloof.

"The first time I photographed her was in 1931, when M.G.M. borrowed her from Howard Hughes for *The Secret Six*. Although she'd made *Hell's Angels* and *The Public Enemy* by that time, she was still a personality rather than a star. When the studio bought out her contract a few months later, she was properly groomed for stardom, and became big box-office. But she never changed personally. She was one star who never, ever believed her publicity.

"Her complexion was creamy and translucent—the envy of every female star on the lot. She took particular pains with her spun-platinum hair. A blonde's coiffure always has more importance than a brunette's, because the lightness catches the light and provides contrast to the face. I also preferred to photograph her in white. A white dress is always more arresting, in the camera and in life. While black is slimming and flatters the figure, men always turn to look at a white-gowned woman. When she dyed her hair to a cinnamon color for *Red Headed Woman*, I found her slightly less interesting to photograph and concentrated more on her vivacious personality.

"She was extremely photogenic, but I always positioned my lights at a low angle, because a top light exaggerated her deep-set eyes, which literally vanished in the camera. I never sought to tone down the slight cleft in her chin, which I found balanced her face.

"She was very sensitive to suggestions. When I posed her in a certain attitude that did not look quite right in my camera, I would say, for instance, 'Change the position of your left hand,' and she would deftly move her palm or her fingers a fraction of an inch without altering the whole effect. She took direction superbly, and I played all sorts of music for her—soft and romantic, loud and raucous—and, consequently, she'd give me a spectrum of moods.

"Harlow was not frightened of the camera; she reacted to it, and in some strange way, I was the third party—*they* were the conspirators."

OVERLEAF:

At the Sunset Boulevard studio. 1935.

At her home. 1934.

A fashion layout, at Bullock's Wilshire store. 1935.

At her home. 1934.

After Red Dust. *1932.*

On the set. 1933.

Johnny Weissmuller

Like wonder dog Rin Tin Tin, over the hills at Warner Bros., there was one actor on the lot who was not concerned about how his voice recorded. If John Gilbert, Ramon Novarro, and Rod La Rocque were on their way out of talking pictures, Johnny Weissmuller, twenty-eight, was very much in—because all he was required to display in *Tarzan the Ape Man* was his magnificent physique and the grace and agility that had earned him some seventy-four world aquatic speed records, including Olympic championships in Paris in 1924 and Amsterdam in 1928. His sole vocal contribution to the audio aspects of the studio was the famous Tarzan yell, which he was still performing on television forty-five years later.

Hurrell was thankful that Norma Shearer had established the precedent of shooting portraits on the sets, because he was able to photograph Weissmuller in a huge, misshapen tree on the jungle back lot. He told Strick: "How can Tarzan be photographed in the still gallery?"

Johnny Weissmuller as Tarzan (Lord Greystoke) in Tarzan the Ape Man. *1932.*

Maureen O'Sullivan

Tarzan's Jane was Maureen O'Sullivan, an Irish lass from County Roscommon. Although she would make some fifty pictures over the next thirty-three years, it was her fate to be remembered during the early years as Tarzan's mate (although they made only six jungle films together) and in later years as Mia Farrow's mother.

The studio requested some "straight stuff" to go along with the two-piece sarong pictures already made. Hurrell posed her, dressed in a Chinese robe, next to an ancient china vase. She was excessively languid, and he felt he was getting very little expression.

He placed a new jazz recording on the Victrola; she did not move an eyelash. Flailing arms and legs in the air, he went into a frantic buck and wing; she examined his tennis shoes. He stood on one leg, with the other leg pointed to the ceiling; she eyed St. Hilaire as he loaded a holder with film. Suddenly, Hurrell got a brilliant idea, and snaked up a nearby ladder to the rafters above. He suspended himself upside down, crossed his eyes, scratched under his armpits, and growled like a monkey; she yawned.

But, quick as a flash, he squeezed the bulb, and caught her calm and interesting face as it lapsed into repose. "That's all," he said. "You can go home now!"

Maureen O'Sullivan before filming Tarzan the Ape Man. *1934.*

OPPOSITE:
Myrna Loy. 1932.

Myrna Loy

Myrna Loy was the most cast-against-type actress in Hollywood in 1933. Eventually she would become known as the "perfect wife" to a string of top box-office men, but her role of Nora Charles in *The Thin Man*, opposite William Powell, was a year away. She had made over fifty feature films, playing every type of role except the one that would make her internationally famous—the slightly daffy, urbane, wholesome, extremely up-to-date woman.

Because of her almond-shaped eyes, she had specialized in Oriental vamp parts, but she had also played half-castes, gangster molls, slave girls, pretty chorines, Indian maidens, and harem beauties, and had even appeared in blackface in *Ham and Eggs at the Front* in 1927.

When Hurrell saw her in street makeup, she looked nothing at all like the Myrna Loy he had seen recently as the perverted daughter in *The Mask of Fu Manchu*. "She had flaming red hair, a small forehead with frown lines that had to be retouched, thousands of freckles, and a pug nose." He recalls, "She had a very dry sense of humor and a husky voice that was very endearing. She also could be completely objective. I lighted her hair very carefully, because her particular shade of red was exceptionally photogenic.

"I alternated fast and slow musical numbers, not only to keep up my own tempo, but to keep her interested in the sitting. She was thoroughly professional and always thanked me after the sessions were over, unlike some of the stars who'd run out the door the moment we were finished. With her great composure, intelligent outlook, and diplomatic manner, I was not in the least surprised when she made a new career for herself in middle age as a member of the National Committee for UNESCO and later at the United Nations."

Grand Hotel

On the way back from lunch at the commissary one day, Hurrell stopped by the *Grand Hotel* set to examine what had become known on the lot as "a piece of Berlin." He was struck with the authenticity of the huge, elegant, Art Deco lobby. The breakaway flats that surrounded him seemed like permanent walls. The romance, the grandeur, the mystique of a famous hostelry was actually communicated to him.

Whenever he was scheduled to shoot portraits on a set, he liked to roam over the sound stage and soak up the atmosphere. He would be shooting for several days, because some of the characters (all with almost impossible-to-pronounce names) did not meet in the screenplay. For instance, Garbo as the premiere danseuse Grusinskaya never encountered Flaemmchen, the little secretary played by Joan Crawford. Among the other guests of the hotel whose individual stories became entwined were: John Barrymore as Baron von Geigern; his brother Lionel as the bookkeeper, Otto Kringelein; Wallace Beery as his tycoon employer, Preysing; Jean Hersholt as Senf the porter.

The all-star film, a precedent for dramatic storytelling, was destined to become one of the studio's biggest box-office hits. Many players were cast against type. Garbo, who was rather big-boned, seemed hardly the delicate type for a ballerina, but she had studied the attitudes of the dance, and was photographed in such a manner that her graceful movements were totally in keeping with the role. Beery had difficulty mastering a German accent, but his great physical bulk and short crewcut helped him be convincing. The brothers Barrymore were more at home with their roles, but it was Crawford who surprised everyone with the intense way she tackled the role. In her autobiography she later wrote: "I was exhausting every resource I had and drawing on ones I didn't know existed. Can you imagine the dancing daughter in a scene with Beery and two Barrymores? The upstaging was historic. John was like Peck's Bad Boy. He was usually 'hung over' and would appear on the set with a shy appealing quality. He would use four-letter words, then giggle like a little boy. But, play ended the instant the camera started rolling. Then he became beauteous and fiery."

Hurrell found the great Barrymore beauteous, but not fiery. "He was thoroughly professional and appeared almost bored. His 'presence' was similar to Chaney's, so strong that all he had to do was lean against a doorway, and I got a study of a man that was already becoming a legend."

Crawford was different, somewhat unsure. Hurrell spoke to her gently. As the music swelled dramatically in the background, she hugged her furs around her, more for professional security than personal warmth, and Flaemmchen, the little whore-stenographer, sprang to life.

Beery and Hersholt were easier to work with, but, wrapped up in their roles, these two kept in character even away from the set.

Garbo was detached, as usual, and yet striking an attitude with Barrymore, there was a certain spark, a flame. Hurrell found himself wondering if she missed another John—Gilbert—who could have had the role if he had been up to it. With the two most famous profiles in the world to pose, he asked Garbo and Barrymore to stand face to face, and suddenly, there was majesty.

John Barrymore as Baron von Geigern in Grand Hotel. *1933.*

John and Lionel Barrymore in Grand Hotel.

Lionel Barrymore

Wallace Beery as the tycoon, Preysing, in Grand Hotel.

OPPOSITE: *Joan Crawford as Flaemmchen in* Grand Hotel.

Joan Crawford and Wallace Beery in Grand Hotel.

Joan Crawford and John Barrymore in Grand Hotel.

OPPOSITE:
Greta Garbo and John Barrymore in Grand Hotel.

Ethel Barrymore in her garden. 1932.

Ethel Barrymore

"I was on vacation when *Rasputin and the Empress* went into production," Hurrell relates, "so missed shooting Ethel, John, and Lionel Barrymore together, but the lot was filled with rumors about all the upstaging that was going on over at Stage 22. To see all the three Barrymores on the set was quite an experience. The studio had re-created the palace of Czar Nicholas right down to the samovars. Miss Barrymore was playing the Czarina, and John the Prince, and both were costumed magnificently. But Lionel as the mad monk Rasputin was something to see, with his long dark wig and straggly beard."

In her autobiography, *Memories*, Ethel Barrymore wrote of her M.G.M. experiences:

Making *Rasputin* with Lionel and Jack was one of the very few times all three of us were together after our early childhood days, but I hardly saw them except at the studio. . . .

Of course there is no truth in the nonsensical publicity stories about quarrels between us that were put out while we were making the picture. We were all actors, working at a job, and besides, we didn't know each other well enough to quarrel. You must remember that we were always very frighteningly polite to each other. Scene stealing between Lionel and Jack was a joke. They did it for fun. . . .

"After the picture was completed, Strick asked me to take portable equipment over to Miss Barrymore's house to shoot stills. I'd only seen her in full makeup and costume on the palace set, regal and beautiful, and so was totally unprepared for the rather plain woman who greeted me at the door. Like her brothers, she had the Barrymore profile. But her most startling feature was her large, extremely lovely eyes that transformed her face.

" 'So nice of you to come, Mr. Hurrell,' she said and her cello-like voice gave me goose bumps. 'I want a few snaps for my family album. My sons are here with me, and we haven't had decent pictures taken together since they were mites.'

"I photographed her in the garden with natural light pouring down through the oak leaves. I was reminded of the time that I'd shot Novarro under the trees at Poncho Barnes's house in San Marino. But I had a whale of a time shooting Miss Barrymore (I could never have called her 'Ethel'). She eventually got her 'snaps.' "

The Barrymore Family. Back row, left to right: John Drew Colt, John Barrymore and Samuel Colt. Front row, left to right: Lionel and Irene (Fenwick) Barrymore and John's son; Ethel Barrymore; Dolores Costello (Mrs. John) Barrymore with daughter, and Ethel Barrymore Colt. 1932.

Joan Crawford

"Joan Crawford was, for many years, the most photogenic of the Hollywood group of actresses," Hurrell recalls. "When we first met, she swept into the gallery full of energy and drama. I reacted immediately to her warmth and her dazzle. Although she came on rather strong, she could be utterly feminine. Many of the female stars whom I photographed every day were of the passive sort, but that could never be said of Crawford. She also had a perfectly proportioned figure, and her one defect—broad shoulders—was turned into an asset by Adrian's costume designs.

"When I caught my first glimpse of her in the lens, I felt an emotional tug of excitement and knew that I had a unique subject. Her brown-reddish hair, large wide eyes, and strongly molded features were perfect in the camera.

"I photographed her literally thousands of times, and each sitting was a new experience for both of us. For one thing, she constantly altered her appearance, the color of her hair, eye makeup, eyebrows, and mouth. Yet, with all the changes, there was a classic beauty, a weird kind of spirituality, if you will, that was always there.

"She appreciated the *theatricality* of my method of working, and she responded to the music in an extraordinary way. She was easy to shoot. A top light was very good, bringing out the lovely modeling in her face. But if light was placed incorrectly, her nostrils appeared larger than they really were. That is because the bridge of her nose was so slender that any glimpse of the nostrils seemed large by contrast."

Hurrell liked to work with very little use of cosmetics. He preferred his female subjects to wear lipstick and eye makeup, because skin texture was lost with a covering of paint. Crawford would scrub her face with soap until it shone before going for a sitting. "Let me worry about your freckles," he told her.

Drive, ambition, and her clothes-horse sense of glamour were no doubt built up by a horrendous childhood. Her early days as a tireless Charleston contest winner, her first painfully performed roles where she was fighting for expression and poise, were the backbone of her challenging career. Her first big break had come when she played Mary Turner in *Paid*, a no-nonsense dramatic role that Shearer had refused because of her pregnancy. From that point on, the dancing daughter became an *actress*, and a big, big box-office star.

Crawford never grew irritated or bored with posing. She was Hurrell's most enthusiastic subject. They made something of a record when he exposed five hundred plates in one sitting. After that session, St. Hilaire collapsed from fatigue after loading so many holders, and Hurrell, completely spent, took off the next day, a Friday, and spent the entire weekend in Carmel painting landscapes.

OPPOSITE: *An unretouched photograph. 1933.*

OVERLEAF: Chained. *1934.*

Dancing Lady. *1933.*

Before Letty Lynton. *1932.*

Before Letty Lynton. *1932.*

Douglas Fairbanks, Jr.

Nineteen-year-old Douglas Fairbanks, Jr., had a polish that was new to the lot. He had charm and an easy courtliness that other male actors had to feign. Douglas Fairbanks, Sr., married to Mary Pickford and famous for his swashbuckling roles, had been well educated, but when the family fortunes dwindled, Doug, Jr., went to work at an early age and received most of his schooling via tutor. But mainly he educated himself by 'burning the midnight oil'. He later wrote articles that were published in national magazines and composed titles for silent films. Eventually, he was honored with several honorary degrees. He formed his own production company and became celebrated for his meritorious service during World War II, receiving many accolades, including the Distinguished Service Cross and the Croix de Guerre.

Hurrell remembers: "I was introduced to Doug, Jr., in 1930 by his then wife, Joan Crawford. They wanted some casual shots together, not posed or dramatic—the sort of photograph that could be framed on the mantel. At that time there was great publicity wherever they went, which I suppose was good for their careers. He was not under contract to M.G.M., although I think he made two pictures on the lot, the last with Crawford, *Our Modern Maidens*, in 1929. He worked mostly for Warner Bros.

"I photographed him many times. Erudite, urbane, and amusing, he would give me the exact mood I wanted. I never put on much of a show for him, although he liked happy, upbeat tunes. I got the impression that although he was awed by his dad's reputation, he wasn't terribly ambitious himself. He was the 'good scout' kind of player."

Douglas Fairbanks, Jr., at his home. 1933.

Clark Gable

The hardest working player on the lot in 1931 was thirty-year-old Clark Gable, with twelve pictures in release. He had started out as a tool dresser in the Oklahoma oil fields and also worked as a lumberjack. "Gable was that rare individual," says Hurrell, "who was a sex symbol for women and, at the same time, a man's man. His following, then, was equally composed of both sexes. He was the fantasy man for females, big, masculine, rough, tough, yet tender and knowing. To males, he was the personification of their own machismo image: this man knew how to handle women, was not afraid to push them around, and yet was a bulwark of comfort when emotional tides turned against them. He was always there, bigger than life.

"In person he looked very much as he did on the screen, but his manner was entirely different: he was almost shy in those early days. He took direction well and knew what was expected of him; he never shirked his professional duties. Gable looked upon the Hollywood scene as a business. He did not know how long his career would last, and he was determined to make the most of every opportunity and collect as much money as possible for his services. He was a pure realist. I remember one day, years later, when he was making *Boomtown* with Spencer Tracy, still dressed in coveralls (the wardrobe for the picture), he and Tracy came out of Strick's office and ran into a group of ladies who were touring the lot. Spence said, 'Let's get out of here,' and dodged around the corner of a sound stage, but Clark stayed to sign autographs.

"We used to have great times together. He was humorous and fun to be around, and he appreciated and was amused by my antics, the 'shows' I put on for different stars. We always cut up when we worked. He would lose his initial tenseness and relax with the music, which was always loud and fast. He never used much makeup and the only trouble Korf had was retouching his very heavy blue-black beard.

"His first big success came about in an unexpected way. Cast as the heavy in *A Free Soul*, he was supposed to elicit sympathy for Norma Shearer by knocking her around. But the tables turned, because of the way females all over the world reacted to his rough treatment; instead of feeling sorry for her, they felt that she *deserved* being treated roughly. It was the Cagney, grapefruit-in-the-face routine all over again.

"Later when Clark became a top box-office star, and became known as 'The King,' he didn't change. If anything, he became more humble."

As it turned out, Gable became the longest reigning contract star at M.G.M., from 1930 to 1955. When he died in 1960 after making *The Misfits* with Marilyn Monroe, and before the birth of his only son, he was still The King.

OPPOSITE: *Clark Gable and Joan Crawford in* Love on the Run. *1936.*

OVERLEAF LEFT: *Clark Gable and Joan Crawford in* Possessed. *1931.*

RIGHT: *Clark Gable. 1932.*

Laurence Olivier. 1933.

Laurence Olivier

Strick was on the phone. "George, I've got a new guy over here that Thalberg's going to use in *Queen Christina* with Garbo. He's a nice enough chap. See what you can do with him."

Hurrell looked quizzically at twenty-six-year-old Laurence Olivier. "He was devilishly handsome with his marcelled hair and tiny moustache. In truth, he resembled a young John Gilbert, who, ironically, replaced him shortly after in the Garbo picture. He was 'teddibly' British and somewhat supercilious. I never expected that this rather formal young man would be knighted by the Queen of England, and turn out to be one of the most respected actors in the world.

"I played popular music, jazz, and even a music-hall piece, but he was old sobersides. I finally settled on several straight poses and asked him to light up a cigarette to give a casual look. He made such a small impression that I'm quite sure I called him *Oliver!*"

OPPOSITE: *Clark Gable. 1934.*

75

Marion Davies

If Norma Shearer had a true rival on the lot, it was Marion Cecilia Douras Davies, the protégée of the powerful William Randolph Hearst, whose Cosmopolitan Pictures was housed at M.G.M. Hurrell seldom photographed Davies, since she had a favorite portrait photographer, but he found her charming, somewhat aloof, and happily lacking the aggressive attitudes that some of the female stars displayed. He appreciated her reticent manner and appealing sincerity.

"Having been Hearst's mistress for well over a decade," Hurrell says, "her public life could not have been easy—which perhaps explained her natural reserve. Her slight stutter incongruously added to her charm."

Usually photographed with acres of ruffles, big picture hats, and golden curls, Hurrell sought to capture a different quality and photographed her in a plain dress with a simple hairdo, and later, quite soberly, in a striking beige riding outfit.

But soon her love affair with M.G.M. grew cold. Denied parts that she felt were rightly hers, like Elizabeth Barrett Browning in *The Barretts of Wimpole Street*, she moved her bungalow *and* her production company to Warner Bros.

Hurrell did not see her again.

Marion Davies. 1933.

Toward the end of 1933, the phantasmagoria of studio life was beginning to pall. Hurrell no longer looked forward with excitement to his day's work, which included a routine of endless sittings, interminable wardrobe changes, continual applications of makeup, endless rearrangements of hair, getting the good side of a face and hiding the bad, and playing hundreds and hundreds of phonograph records. With the pace, the tension, the concentration, the repeated trips to the rooftop for a breath of fresh air, the gallery was becoming a prison.

One Sunday morning he went to Malibu to photograph Lilyan Tashman. A friend, publicity woman Maggie Ettinger, had asked for art on client Tashman, who was then making a picture at RKO. On Monday morning, Hurrell brought in the films for St. Hilaire to develop. Through the spy network that was rampant at M.G.M., word reached Strick about the Tashman job. The publicity man accosted Hurrell on his way to lunch. "What do you mean using the studio facility for outside work?" he demanded. "Doing a job on our time!"

Hurrell was flabbergasted. The argument became heated and both men lost their tempers. "Look," Hurrell shouted angrily, "I've had this job up to my ears. I'll leave *now*."

"Where will you go?" Strick expostulated. "If you leave M.G.M., you will be unemployable. No other studio will touch you with a ten-foot pole!"

"That's all right with me! I'd rather go on WPA than take this kind of crap." He paused, then came up with what he felt was the clincher. "In fact, I may open my own studio."

"You're a fool, George. Whom would you photograph?" Strick smiled coldly. "People off the street? What would the ordinary person make of your crazy ways? Independent portrait guys don't get anywhere in this town. You'd better give up."

"Never!"

Hurrell turned furiously and literally ran up the three flights to the gallery to pick up his belongings. When St. Hilaire and Korf learned of the altercation, they also packed, and a few moments later the trio walked out the front gate of Metro-Goldwyn-Mayer.

But Hurrell's M.G.M. story had one last, glorious chapter. One week after Hurrell had stomped off the lot, the telephone rang. It was Strick on the other end of the line. The publicity man's voice was not unfriendly. "What are you doing?"

"I'm completing a charcoal sketch," Hurrell replied guardedly, "and resting. Why?" He decided in that split second before Strick answered that he would return to the studio only with the condition that his salary be raised to $700—double what he had been getting.

There was a long pause and then Strick went on, with some difficulty. "Norma Shearer's back on the lot. . . . She needs . . . some new shots . . ."

"Yes?" Hurrell said brightly. "Yes?"

"Well, why don't you come out . . . and, well, shoot the stuff—on an independent basis, of course."

"Oh all right," Hurrell replied. "Of course."

"How much?"

Hurrell made fast calculations. "Twenty negs for two hundred dollars."

"My God!" Strick exploded. "That's highway robbery!"

Hurrell sighed, "That's only ten bucks each. If that's going to break the studio, then I suggest you get someone else."

There was a long pause. Hurrell knew exactly what was going through Strick's mind. Miss Norma Shearer had made a request. It was a command from the Queen. "All right, all right. Come on out and shoot the stuff."

The relationship was strained beween the two men for some time. However, with the passing of the years, the rancor faded and a new, mellow camaraderie developed. They became friends once more.

Independent

Hurrell returned from the Shearer sitting at M.G.M. more determined than ever to establish his own studio. He did not want a private atelier similar to the old Lafayette Park Place town house, but a modern building on a busy street that would have a great deal of foot traffic. He found the perfect location at 8706 Sunset Boulevard, quite near his apartment on Fountain Avenue.

The storefront was only about 12 feet wide, but was extremely long. There was room for a dressing room and bath. He first thought that a marquee would dress up the exterior of the building, but then his painter's eye took over and he visualized a huge, glass-enclosed picture frame to contain the portrait of his latest subject. The frame turned out to be 9½ feet long and 6 feet wide, which would allow for a 5 x 7 foot photograph to be mounted inside. It covered the entire front of the building. Between the lease on the studio and the cost of the huge photograph of Norma Shearer in the outside frame, his bank account was depleted.

He borrowed eight hundred dollars from Maggie Ettinger's husband, painter Ross Shattuck, and purchased several juniors, seniors, and broads. He had a new boom light built to order. Then he bought an 8 x 10 portable view camera (with a swinging head and a three-legged tripod) on the installment plan. St. Hilaire, back from vacation in the East, was employed as assistant. A secretary-receptionist was hired, and Andrew Korf offered to do retouching at home on a free-lance basis. Hurrell was ready for business.

All the equipment and props were in readiness, including his huge white polar-bear rug. Standing in the middle of the new studio, he experienced a moment of panic. Why had he taken this incredibly foolish step? He had worked for a paycheck for three years and had grown accustomed to spending money without thought. Now he was charging two hundred and fifty dollars for a sitting, for twelve finished negs and twelve 11 x 14 prints. Could he *really* survive in a town overrun with still photographers?

The next day he and Poncho Barnes went to the Brown Derby for lunch. Hurrell was not even sure he could get a booth, now that he did not have a studio connection.

But the maitre d' was all smiles and as he led them to a front booth, greetings poured in from all sides. Lilyan Tashman and Edmund Lowe were the first; then Jimmy Durante, who waved his napkin wildly in the air. Melvyn Douglas, who had always been rather cold, smiled; and Jackie Cooper, who was with his mother, said: "Hiya, Mr. Hurrell." Dorothy Jordan came over from a back booth to say a few words. Hurrell's sagging spirits rose. Perhaps Strick's prediction would not come true.

The next morning, Hurrell arrived at the studio late. In a flurry of excitement, his secretary handed him a stack of notes. RKO, Paramount, and Twentieth Century-Fox had called. Joan Crawford had telephoned *twice*. He might yet have a future in the business.

One evening, Hurrell was invited to a cocktail party at the Wilshire Boulevard residence of director Frank Borzage. Among the guests was Katherine Cuddy, a beautiful beauty-contest winner from Seattle. There was an immediate, electric attraction. Consequently, they became an "item" around town and were frequently seen on the party circuit. During the summer, they eloped to Santa Barbara and were married. But Hurrell had so many appointments set up that a leisurely honeymoon was impossible. He went back to work immediately.

From time to time, Hurrell received inquiries about photographing in the East. Feeling the need for a change, he and Katherine took off for New York City. He took a month's lease on a studio on the mezzanine of the Sherry Netherlands Hotel on Fifth Avenue, and the next day set up a display of his famous movie-star shots in the front window.

Besides shooting several socialites, he photographed a fashion layout for Bergdorf Goodman, and did a job for Elizabeth Arden cosmetics. The change in routine was most welcome. It was a pleasure to work with models who were malleable, who would pose as he directed without interjecting any bright ideas on how they should be shot. He found he liked commercial work, and would continue to accept such assignments throughout his career. In 1936, he also became a regular contributor to *Esquire* magazine, doing a series of portraits of women stars.

Constance Bennett

Constance Bennett, whom Hurrell photographed many times, was called the highest paid actress in the world during the early 1930s, when she was getting $30,000 a week. "She was always the same," Hurrell remem-

bers, "in love or not, hair long or short, in my studio or on the set—a very witty, sophisticated in-tune-with-the-times lady. She'd just finished *After Office Hours* at M.G.M. with Clark Gable when she came to the Sunset Boulevard Studio with her new husband, the Marquis de la Falaise, who had formerly been married to Gloria Swanson. But Constance was especially effervescent with the Marquis, who was a regular guy. I photographed her later with Gilbert Roland, when she was married to him. It took some doing in those days to remember who was married to whom, especially when star sittings might be several years between!

"She greeted me like an old friend. I played soft, romantic music and she struck several unusual poses, giggling between shots. Her blond hair was especially photogenic, and she had an excellent profile and a neck that looked swanlike when thrust back. It's easy to photograph a woman in love. There's a softness and vulnerability that is quite touching. A man often hides these feelings, but a woman wears them like a light. Constance Bennett was a beacon light that day on Sunset."

Luise Rainer

On one of his numerous trips back to M.G.M., Hurrell was introduced to Luise Rainer, a tiny, shy import, who had studied with Max Reinhardt in Berlin, and had made a few German films before coming to the United States in 1935. She was extraordinarily pretty, with a mop of black, rather short hair, worn in casual bangs that was her offscreen trademark. She had a breathless kind of voice, soft and light, and she spoke with an intriguing Viennese accent.

Hurrell played soaring, romantic music. Because she was somewhat like a fragile flower, he had a dozen white gladiolas—which she pronounced *glad-i-loves*—brought on the set. She never felt she was a glamour girl and refused to be shot in a bathing suit or a revealing low-cut gown.

Although Rainer was to make only eight films for M.G.M., she would win two Academy Awards in succession, as Anna Held in *The Great Ziegfeld* in 1936, and as O-Lan in *The Good Earth* in 1937. But her extreme sensitivity worked against her. She refused to be incorporated into the studio system, and her fire soon faded out and she went into retirement.

Luise Rainer. 1935.

Rosalind Russell

Rosalind Russell was placed under contract at M.G.M. in 1934. A tall, intelligent, energetic, outdoorsy woman, she had been well educated (Barnard College), and her bright conversation reflected her excellent upbringing. She played small parts in several films, beginning with *Evelyn Prentice*, and her role as the "other woman" in *China Seas* in 1935, with Jean Harlow and Clark Gable, was very well received. She was frequently loaned to other studios, but it was *Craig's Wife*, at Columbia in 1936, that proved the turning point in her career. Later, she won four Academy Award nominations for *My Sister Eileen* (1942), *Sister Kenny* (1946), *Mourning Becomes Electra* (1947), and *Auntie Mame* (1958).

As Myrna Loy became famous as the "perfect wife," Rosalind Russell became renowned for her "woman executive" role, a part she played in twenty-three films. Although she had "aged" in *Roughly Speaking* in 1945 and *Sister Kenny*, in 1946, her first all-out character part was the frustrated spinster in *Picnic* in 1956, when she was forty-four. Two years later she transferred her Broadway hit *Auntie Mame* to the screen, and it became her most memorable portrait.

"The first time I saw Roz," smiles Hurrell, "she was getting out of her old Ford convertible on the M.G.M. lot. She wore a beret and her wool suit was covered with dog hair. She and the mutts lived in a cottage in the Beachwood Drive area, near the *Hollywoodland* sign. I liked her very much. Her personality and drive were very impressive, although I think she felt a bit intimidated by the glamorous female stars on the lot. One of the first times I photographed her was on the set, and she was dressed to the teeth. The amazing thing about Roz was that she became the character of the costume she was wearing. She was very soignée that day. After we were finished, she announced, 'I must change and go see Mr. Mayer. I've just read a script I've simply *got* to do!' and she was off, gown and fur flying. She could walk so fast that most people had a time keeping up with her.

"She was the leading bachelor girl in Hollywood for a long time, but when she married Frederick Brisson, her life changed completely. She became a great hostess and very involved in social activities.

"She was entertained by my singing and dancing, and our sittings were always fun. But I liked the dramatic shots best, where she became sultry and dreamy. She always examined the proofs with great attention to detail, and we would discuss retouching as if planning major surgery.

"But when I think of Roz today, it is not the lady involved in philanthropies, but that young girl in the beret and wool suit, with the dogs in the front seat of her old Ford, driving off the lot and waving gaily to the gateman."

Rosalind Russell wears a silver-lamé-and-fox creation by Adrian. 1935.

Rosalind Russell poses for a Hurrell Esquire *magazine shot. 1940.*

Adrian

Gilbert Adrian, M.G.M.'s top dress designer, who had influenced more fashion trends than his Parisian coutourier cousins, lived in an apartment at the quaint, rambling French Village, situated across from the Hollywood Bowl. Hurrell recalls: "He so disliked having to be photographed that he refused to come to the studio gallery. Once I had shot him in his large offices, with sketches piled everywhere, but Strick had insisted that he have new portraits made." Adrian grudgingly gave in—but only if Hurrell would come to the French Village.

"I was greeted by six dachshunds," Hurrell laughs, "all yipping and yapping and jumping up over my equipment. Adrian finally banished them to the bathroom so we could have some peace and quiet."

Adrian nervously paced the floor. "Let's get this over with, George. God, I deplore this sort of thing. What can you do to this face? I look exactly like a moose!"

Hurrell smiled. "Just sit in that chair and look off into space."

He threw himself in the chair, cringing, then jumped up again. "Aren't you finished yet?" He asked nervously.

"Not quite!"

Adrian resumed his position, his long legs thrust out in front of him. Hurrell sighed, knowing it was impossible to get the expression that he wanted. He decided to let the lighting provide the effect. He quickly shot several films, keeping the left side of Adrian's face in shadow to create an interesting feeling.

After ten minutes, Adrian jumped out of the chair, crying "Enough! Enough!" and rushed to the bathroom, inadvertently freeing the dogs, which again started to nip at Hurrell's legs. "I quickly gathered my equipment together as best I could," says Hurrell, "and fled into the courtyard, the bitches running after me, barking up a storm. As I got into my car, I saw 'the moose' chasing the animals, trying to gather them, unsuccessfully, into his arms. I was so unnerved, I took the rest of the day off."

Adrian. 1936.

Tallulah Bankhead

The voice on the other end of the line was unmistakable. "Mr. Hurrell, this is Tallulah Bankhead. I'm in town for a few weeks and I need some new photographs. I'll bring along some gowns, but I want to ask your advice about makeup."

Tallulah Bankhead. 1936.

"As little as possible, please. Lipstick and eye makeup, and that's about it."

"Fine. Is it possible to have an afternoon engagement? I really don't function in the morning."

"Of course." An appointment was set up. Hurrell was enthusiastic about shooting her: "She had such a wild reputation that I was fully prepared for a madcap, freewheeling kind of sitting. In fact, I found her rather preoccupied." He was reminded of the furor connected with her last picture, *Faithless*, in Hollywood, at M.G.M. four years before. During the shooting of the film she had given up smoking and drinking, but she could not discipline herself for very long, apparently, because she had given an interview to Gladys Hall of *Motion Picture* magazine that had curled everyone's hair. "It had to do with, to put it delicately," Hurrell smiles, "her lack of male companionship, and caused tremors at the studio."

But now she was concerned only about her appearance. "Don't fret," he told her, "let me worry about how you look." He had acquired some interesting props to add a bit of opulence. He posed her on a rather ornate chair and began to shoot.

"Let me know when you are ready, Mr. Hurrell," she said.

He laughed. "I've already shot half a dozen."

"What? I haven't seen you 'under the hood.' "

"I don't work that way," he explained gently. "I line you up in the camera, my assistant attends to the focusing, and that's it!" He shot her in a number of attitudes, but the one he liked best was a shot before an ornate mirror, a kind of narcissistic pose. "She liked the proofs immensely," Hurrell says, "But come to think of it, as I look back over the rather sedate sitting, she never once called me '*Dahrling*'!"

Gloria Vanderbilt

"*Vogue* magazine called to see if I was free to take a color shot of Gloria Vanderbilt, one of the new bright debutantes. I brought my equipment to her rented house in Beverly Hills. She was friendly, but had the genteel façade that I encountered only with persons of great wealth. Because her gown and hairdo were a bit overwhelming, I posed her in a huge chair to place her in proper proportion. The sitting went well. When I thanked her and she extended her hand and smiled, I had the distinct impression that I was standing in a reception line."

Gloria Vanderbilt.

Robert Taylor

Despite Robert Taylor's image as a ladies' man, he loved the outdoors. He was more at home fishing, riding, and skeet shooting than on a sound stage. His first picture was *Handy Andy*, starring Will Rogers, in 1934. It was made at Twentieth Century-Fox on loan out from M.G.M.—where he was to stay for twenty years. He played opposite virtually every star on the lot, including Garbo in *Camille*.

"Bob Taylor was not the ambitious type," says Hurrell. "He was never at the front office fighting for roles. He did the best he could with his assignments, and then enjoyed his life at his ranch. I shot him many times over the years, when he was married to Barbara Stanwyck and later to Ursula Thiess. Whether wearing a moustache or not, he had a great photographic face and he aged well. As he was a superb horseman, it was natural that he eventually did so many westerns.

"He was very casual about his good looks. He was equally good in full face, three-quarters or profile. Because of his fine build, I always thought he looked better in costume stuff. When I'd show up at the ranch for a sitting, we would gab about where the salmon were running, the chances of bagging a deer up at Bishop or how his tennis game was improving. He was a delightful guy."

William Powell

William Powell, who made his first picture in 1920, had one of the longest careers in Hollywood, making around ninety films. Never typed, he played mainly villains in the silent era and detectives in the thirties, but he could also expertly perform romantic and high-comedy roles. His *Thin Man* series with Myrna Loy established him as a sophisticated, urbane type with bright lines and double takes. His last picture was *Mister Roberts* in 1955, after which he retired to Palm Springs.

"Bill Powell wasn't conventionally handsome," says Hurrell. "He had big features and a wide smile, and was one of the most impeccably groomed men I ever photographed. He was always in such good humor that I really looked forward to his sittings. I played loud, hot swing music and hollered and danced and tore my hair, breaking him up time after time. He hated stiff poses because he'd been photographed soberly when playing 'heavies' early in his career.

"He was very much in love with Jean Harlow and her death was a tremendous blow. I remember he telephoned me at that time; I hardly recognized his voice. The underlying, mocking tone was gone, and he sounded strained and wounded. Knowing that I'd photographed Harlow so often, he asked me to send over several of my best shots, which I was very pleased to do. He took a bit of time off from acting, and when I photographed him again, I had to work twice as hard to break him up. He was different—more mature, I guess; but he was still responsive to the camera, and to me."

William Powell before the start of The Great Ziegfeld. *1936.*

Robert Taylor. 1936.

*Franchot Tone
at the M.G.M. gallery. 1937.*

Franchot Tone

Franchot Tone was married to Joan Crawford when Hurrell first photographed him.

"Franchot was basically an intellectual," Hurrell says, "and his good schooling and social background were obvious to everyone. He was a gentle man. He had an easygoing charm, and his personality was never forced. His quizzical smile was interesting, but it was necessary to keep him amused or, like Shirley Temple, he would drift off into boredom. In movies he often seemed the fifth wheel, as he was usually cast opposite very strong female stars like Joan Crawford, Katharine Hepburn, Jean Harlow, or Bette Davis."

Miriam Hopkins

Miriam Hopkins after the filming of The Woman I Love. *1937.*

As if making a whirlwind entrance on a movie set, expensive perfume preceding her arrival, Miriam Hopkins swept into the Sunset Boulevard studio, whisked by the receptionist, and floated up to Hurrell. She stretched out her hand and started to speak in her soft Georgia-cracker drawl. "So good to see you again, George. I've just had my hair done. Sorry I'm late. The picture at Goldwyn's finished. I hope I don't get an eye infection from this new mascara. Willie Wyler is a great director, but *hard, hard.* I had lunch yesterday at the Brown Derby with an English friend. Do you think I've got too much lipstick on? I may go over there to do a picture with Alexander Korda. My God, what *is* that music, it's so familiar. Do you know I've never been photographed on a bearskin rug? I brought along a little black dress because I want to look svelte. . . ."

"She had a certain vibrancy," Hurrell remembers, "that was evident even when she was in repose—which was not often. She liked the sound of her own voice. Her nervous energy, so effective in front of the movie camera, was also very apparent in my still camera. She was never static. I worked very quickly because her energy was so tremendous that a long sitting would wear me out, while she was about as depleted as a prize fighter going into the ring for his first round!"

Charles Laughton

Charles Laughton. 1937.

"Laughton had an obsession about his chin," Hurrell recalls with a laugh, "and he felt it would look stronger if partially covered, so he'd sneak his hand into the shot. I explained that this was not at all necessary, that lighting would take care of the imagined defect. But he was a man of strong convictions. He could be quite jovial and witty offscreen, but as a serious actor, he objected to 'teeth shots.' Once in a while, if I stood on my hands, I might get a small, bemused smile."

Laughton was a character actor from the beginning. Because of his size and his solid, ordinary looks, he was not the matinee-idol type ("Thank God!" he once exclaimed). While his array of historical characters was impressive (Nero, Henry VIII, Rembrandt, Claudius, Herod), so were his comedy films. On the heels of his splendid performance as Elizabeth Barrett's father in *The Barretts of Wimpole Street* in 1934, three hit films were released the next year, his most impressive career achievement. These were the impeccable English butler, Marmaduke Ruggles, transferred to the Old West in *Ruggles of Red Gap;* Inspector Javert, who tracked down Jean Valjean so mercilessly in *Les Misérables;* and the imperious Captain Bligh in *Mutiny on the Bounty.*

OPPOSITE: *Spencer Tracy. 1936.*

OPPOSITE BELOW: *Spencer Tracy and Jean Harlow in* Libeled Lady. *1936.*

Elsa Lanchester

Elsa Lanchester. 1937.

Elsa Lanchester, whom Charles Laughton married in 1929, was also a character actress from the beginning. She could do both comedy and drama or a combination of the two and, strangely, worked more as she grew older than in the 1930s, when she often appeared in small roles in her husband's films. She created the monster's mate in 1935 in *The Bride of Frankenstein,* a film that has reached cult status. A fey, humorous woman with an engaging singing voice and a gift for mimicry, she could portray with equal virtuosity the delightful Anne of Cleves in *The Private Life of Henry VIII* in 1933, and the squirrelly witch in *Bell, Book, and Candle* in 1958.

"Elsa was delightful," Hurrell says. "She was a perfect foil for her husband. And while Charles was not impressed with my shenanigans, she literally screamed with laughter and, like Jimmy Durante, implied I was giving her competition. She had great legs. We worked out a gag shot—a sexy pose that was even more incongruous because she wore a boy's cap, an old moth-eaten sweater, a rather long skirt, which she hiked up, and very expensive high-heeled shoes. We clowned so much that her husband went out for a walk on Sunset. At one point, she wanted me to pose and ran around behind the camera and ducked her head under the hood, while St. Hilaire and I completely broke up. It was a memorable day."

Spencer Tracy

"Spencer Tracy was a complete individualist," recalls Hurrell. "He was a fine, expressive actor before the motion-picture camera, but he disliked taking the time to be photographed for still shots. He'd come into the gallery with a pained expression on his face. But once he settled into posing, I always thought he rather enjoyed the experience. He felt he was not a glamour personality. Although we never discussed it, he possessed more true inner spark than many of the so-called pretty boys. I'd think he was giving me very little expression, but he would turn on an inner time clock, with the result that the photographs always showed he was *thinking*—very valuable to a photographer. When he posed with women, he was responsive in an entirely different manner. When I shot him and Jean Harlow in 1936 and he drew her close, there was a tenderness expressed that was very touching."

Katharine Hepburn

Katharine Hepburn. 1941.

"I had never seen anyone quite like Katharine Hepburn before," recalls Hurrell. "I only photographed her twice, once when she was under contract to RKO and again later at M.G.M. The first was a magazine assignment, showing her wearing some jewels from Paul Flato. She came striding into my studio in slacks and a corduroy coat, carrying a black velvet evening dress over one arm. 'It will take me only a moment to change,' she said in that peculiar Bryn Mawr accent. I hadn't even had time to adjust my light when she came out of the dressing room. 'I'm ready,' she said. 'Where do you want me? I think maybe if I sat in a chair where I would be comfortable, it might be better. I don't like being photographed, so it helps if I can have some support to my back.' She chatted on and on, a vibrant, take-command lady.

"When I played 'Lulu's Back in Town,' she brightened up and laughed. 'Don't you have anything more up-to-date?' I played 'Slumming on Park Avenue' and she broke up. When quiet had been restored, she adjusted the diamond and topaz bracelet and ring. 'I suppose you'll want my hands in this,' she said, and I agreed that since the photographs were to feature the jewelry, it would be a good idea. We worked quickly. Before I had time to turn off my lamps, she had changed. She waved at the door, then strode down Sunset. St. Hilaire looked at me. We both had the same reaction: 'Whew!'"

Katharine Hepburn with jewels by Paul Flato. 1937.

Mary Pickford & Buddy Rogers

When Joan Crawford was still married to Douglas Fairbanks, Jr., she had shown several of her Hurrell portraits to Mary Pickford, who was entranced. "I wish I could look like that. I wonder what he could do with me?" An appointment was arranged. Mary Pickford, the first motion-picture star, the first person in the world to have her name above the title of a film, and "America's Sweetheart" by unanimous proclamation, sat for Hurrell. She was delighted with the results, because he photographed her like the mature woman that she was, and not the little girl that audiences had cherished for decades. She had finally grown up, at the age of thirty-six, in *Coquette,* for which she had won an Academy Award in 1930, after her two adult roles in *Rosita* and *Dorothy Vernon of Hadden Hall* had proven light at the box office.

Years passed. Pickford's last film, *Secrets,* with Leslie Howard, was released in March of 1933. Douglas Fairbanks Sr. and she were divorced in January of 1936, and she married Charles Edward 'Buddy' Rogers in June the following year. Shortly after the ceremony, Buddy Rogers called Hurrell. "George, Mary and I need a formal picture. Can we come to the studio?"

The sitting went well. They posed on a couch, which Hurrell back-lighted dramatically. After the proofs had been returned, Pickford asked Hurrell to come to "the house" to shoot more portraits.

"The house" was the legendary Pickfair, located on a hill, surrounded by a white cement fence, off Benedict Canyon on Summitridge Drive. The most famous estate in Beverly Hills, Pickfair was a large, rambling, comfortable house with enormous manicured grounds and a large swimming pool.

Hurrell and St. Hilaire drove through the gates, up the drive, under the porte-cochere, and parked near the garages. They were admitted by the butler, followed by Rogers, who asked them to set up the equipment in the drawing room. The decor and the furnishings of the house reflected the Pickford personality—quiet, extremely tasteful, and very feminine. It was an elegant house, and a peaceful aura surrounded it, far removed in feeling from a flossy motion-picture set. Hurrell responded to the subdued atmosphere: he could relax in this environment, and time would pass quickly.

Mary Pickford wore what she referred to as a "nice little black dress" and posed next to a window. The light streaming in through the marquisette curtains turned her blond head into a halo.

"Miss Pickford," Hurrell remembers, "was a good subject, and her innate graciousness came through in her portraits. Her eyes and mouth were the features to be played up, but a three-quarters view was, per-

Mary Pickford and Charles Edward "Buddy" Rogers. 1937.

haps, best. The only angle to be avoided was when she looked downward; then her face seemed too narrow, and the appealing natural fullness was lost.

He asked her to sit near a large vase of giant white chrysanthemums. He angled the camera in for a closeup. As she turned to the window, he saw that she had an exquisite neck. At forty-four, her face had none of the tell-tale wrinkles of most women of her age group. "Miss Pickford," he said, "I would like to shoot you in profile. Just turn to the flowers and raise your chin a trifle. Yes, that's great—stunning." After he took several films, she changed into another black dress, trimmed with ermine, to which she added a string of perfectly matched pearls.

Observing this beautiful woman in her own setting, he regretted that fans had never accepted her as an adult performer. To them, she would always be "Little Mary," the child with the long golden curls.

OPPOSITE: *Mary Pickford. 1937.*

Eleanor Roosevelt. 1937.

Eleanor Roosevelt

"I had exactly seven minutes in which to photograph Eleanor Roosevelt," Hurrell says. "The sitting, arranged by *Junior League* magazine, was scheduled at the home of Mrs. Franklin K. Lane, Jr. We arrived early to set up the lights and camera. Exactly on time, Mrs. Roosevelt came in, dressed in the blue lace dress and a corsage that she would wear at a party later. 'So nice to meet you, Mr. Hurrell,' she said in that distinctive voice that reminded me so much of Ethel Barrymore. 'For a lady who said she was through having photographs taken,' she laughed, 'I seem to be doing pretty well lately.'

"Newspaper photos and candid shots were very unkind to her. In fact, she was not difficult to photograph at all. The secret was in the lighting. Then, too, she wore only powder and light lipstick, so the natural shine of her complexion came through. Newsreel movies often showed her in hats that threw shadows over her best feature, her eyes. She had great poise. Although her time schedule was so tight, she sat down and immediately relaxed as if she had all day to pose. I took several exposures, she thanked me, and left. A few weeks later I received a note saying that she thought the photographs were some of the best ever taken of her.

"I was so proud of the finished product that I made a giant blowup, and placed it in the display frame outside of the studio that had previously held a glamour shot of Jean Harlow. It happened that President Roosevelt came to Los Angeles in the wake of his wife, and his motorcade traveled down Sunset. My staff and I dashed out to the sidewalk to glimpse the president—just as he glimpsed the blowup of his wife. He yelled 'halt,' the limousine stopped, and the half-mile procession closed up. The president stretched his neck in the direction of the picture and broke into a one-sided grin. He gave a low, roguish whistle, then turned to an aide. 'Dear Eleanor,' he whispered. 'Where do you suppose she is at this very minute?' And the motorcade moved on."

Cecil B. De Mille in his office at Paramount. 1938.

PARAMOUNT

Paramount Pictures Corp. had been founded in 1914 by five major stock exchange men: Hiram Abrams of Boston, W. W. Hodkinson of New York, Raymond Pawley of Philadelphia, W. L. Sherry of New York, and James Steele of Pittsburgh. The famous logo of the Rocky Mountains against a cloudy sky was first sketched on a blotter by Hodkinson, and the name Paramount was taken from an apartment building. Despite its humble beginning, the name of Paramount Pictures took on added luster as the years passed. It was now a major studio with an important string of players: Mae West, Cary Grant, Ray Milland, Paulette Goddard, George Raft, Claudette Colbert, Bing Crosby, Bob Hope, Gary Cooper, Dorothy Lamour, and Fred MacMurray.

Carole Lombard

Carole Lombard, blond, beautiful, and bombastic, stood in the middle of the living-room set for *Bolero*, with a cup of coffee in one hand and a script in the other. As usual, the air was blue from her language.

St. Hilaire hung a piece of cellophane over a nearby scenery flat, and arranged the lights. Lombard was dressed in a low-cut, slinky, black dress. Hurrell posed her against the cellophane, which crackled as she sat down. She stuck her tongue out and thumbed her nose at him while St. Hilaire adjusted the key light. Hurrell was used to her chameleonlike changes of mood, as well as her vocabulary, and pressed the bulb. Her cerulean-blue eyes were large and expressive, her creamy complexion

marred only slightly by a thin, hairline scar (which Korf would retouch) running from the corner of her mouth up through the left side of her cheek. Her hair, shimmering in the light, heightened her heart-shaped face. He took several more films.

"Carole was one of my favorite subjects," Hurrell comments. "She could be carrying on like Faust one moment, and then strike an ultradramatic attitude the next. She was always in high spirits, and even when she was swearing up a storm, no one minded, because it was done in such a funny, lowbrow way. The technicians on her pictures truly loved her, and she was so bright and so witty that I always looked forward not only to photographing her, but to just being with her. No one could possibly be bored in her presence."

The last time he photographed Lombard was in 1939, after she had married Clark Gable. She came to the Sunset Boulevard studio with a makeup girl, a hairdresser, and an armload of evening gowns. The session was, again, a strange mixture of dramatic poses and profane language, even more inventive than before.

Three years later, Lombard would be killed in a plane crash as she returned to Hollywood from a triumphant War Bond tour.

Marlene Dietrich

Ernest Hemingway once said of Marlene Dietrich, "If she had only her voice, she would break your heart." It was true: her voice was as responsible for her career as was her beauty. She created in tone and manner a variety of unchaste ladies, who, if lacking hearts of gold, at least totally understood the foibles of man. Her mentor, Josef von Sternberg, wholly created her image, beginning with *Morocco* and *The Blue Angel* in 1930. The magic lasted through five other pictures. Von Sternberg, a martinet, placed her with stunning visual effect in the foreground of his films. Attired in furs, feathers, laces, and beads, she sang and smiled and laughed through gauzy closeups. But she had greater depth than critics imagined, and several of her subsequent films revealed her talents. In *Destry Rides Again* (1939), she showed a remarkable flair for comedy. *A Foreign Affair* in 1948 was a telling drama laid in immediate postwar Berlin, and in *Witness for the Prosecution*, in 1958, she did fine things with a dual role.

"The first time I saw Marlene was on a set at Paramount," Hurrell recalls. "She paused on a staircase between camera setups and looked casually over the crowd of technicians. In a glance, she knew what every one of those sixty-five men was doing and why! She was, no doubt, plan-

OPPOSITE: *Marlene Dietrich liked this shot so much, she spread the proofs from the sitting all around her chair.*

ning what she would do in the next scene. Everything with her was preconceived and studied.

"I shot her many times. All of the sessions were very long, with many costume changes and several different hairdos. She felt that she knew exactly what was right for her. She would assume a pose, check herself in a mirror, and say: 'All right, George, *shoot!*' And I shot. She was the total perfectionist. It was no use trying to catch her off guard—there was no such thing with Marlene. Everything was studied. Still, I must admit, the results were some of the best shots I had ever taken.

"Years later, when she was performing in nightclubs, I did a sitting with her. She was the same polite, concerned woman. Her bone structure still took the light as it had in the old days. But when she returned the proofs to me, they were marked all over with fine lines, indicating what should be removed by the retoucher. She shook her head sadly, 'You don't take pictures like you used to, George.' 'But Marlene,' I said, and also shook my head sadly, 'I'm fifteen years older!' "

Claudette Colbert

Claudette Colbert could be long-suffering, valiant, and noble in one film and gay, laughing, and extroverted in the next. Her real name was Lily Cauchoin. Born in Paris, in 1905, she spoke both English and French fluently. Her first films, beginning in 1927, were barely serviceable, and not until she played Poppaea in *The Sign of the Cross* for Cecil B. De Mille (1932) did she show that she might have a long career—which she did, indeed, until 1961.

She won her first and only Academy Award in 1934 for a comedy, *It Happened One Night*, with Clark Gable. The film was made for a minor company, Columbia Pictures, while she was under contract to Paramount. She had not wanted to do the film, but when director Frank Capra offered her $50,000—double her usual salary per picture—and promised to finish shooting in thirty days, she accepted. The film was done during the vacation due under her Paramount contract. Gable was in the picture only because he had asked for a raise at M.G.M. Louis B. Mayer loaned him to "Gower Gulch" as a punishment. The stars had no faith in the script and performed their roles in a freewheeling, off-the-cuff manner, which turned out to be exactly right for the farcical shenanigans.

The picture did more for both Colbert and Gable than any of the studied roles performed before that time.

"Claudette was one of those 'take charge' people," reveals Hurell. "To her, photographs and publicity interviews were simply a part of the business. She didn't consider posing a favorite pastime. I don't mean to say that she went about it with grim determination, but she didn't have the enthusiasm of a Crawford, the humor of a Lombard, or the dedication of a Harlow.

"Much has been said—and it's all true—about her obsession with the right side of her face, which she always showed as little as possible. Its proportions were slightly different from the left side's, but faces are seldom perfect. If she was to make an entrance in a picture, sets were built to accommodate her coming in from the left. John Barrymore also always turned his left profile to the camera, but he never went to the lengths she did.

"Lighting her very carefully, I sometimes shot the right side of her face, and the photographs turned out very good. She would politely look over the prints, shrug her shoulders, and toss them away. A top light which flattered her apple cheeks was always best for her. Since she always wore simple hairdos and conservative clothing, her photographs did not age. From 1934 to 1954, it is difficult to tell in which year the various shots were taken."

Claudette Colbert. 1938.

Charles Boyer

Charles Boyer. 1936.

"Charles Boyer had a new toupee the first time I shot him," Hurrell confides, "and he was very concerned that the 'lace' around the hairline would show. I told him not to worry, and the sitting commenced. Like George Raft, he was sobersides. Beautiful men are sometimes difficult to photograph, but he wasn't a problem. I don't believe he liked his laugh very much, because he wanted serious poses only."

"I played soft music for him, but didn't put on much of an act. He would change clothing automatically, then pose with a certain amount of grace. He examined the proofs very carefully. The only time he really smiled was when he discovered a particularly good shot that he liked."

Boyer, born in Figeac, France, in 1897, made his first film in 1920 (*L'Homme du Large*) and had a mild career before M.G.M. brought him to America to do French versions of *The Trial of Mary Dugan* and *The Big House* in 1930. Thereafter, he played the chauffeur in *Red Headed Woman* with Jean Harlow. He made starring films for the German UFA Company, and when director Fritz Lang escaped to France from the Hitler menace, he asked Boyer to play the lead in Ferenc Molnar's *Liliom* (1934). Boyer then became leading man to Claudette Colbert, Marlene Dietrich, Katharine Hepburn, Loretta Young, Greta Garbo, Irene Dunne, Bette Davis, Margaret Sullivan, Jennifer Jones, and Ingrid Bergman.

Anna May Wong

Anna May Wong was the only major Chinese actress to achieve stardom in the 1920s and 1930s. She made a comeback many years later, in the late '40s.

Hurrell says, "Anna May Wong was thoroughly businesslike. She brought along an exotic Chinese costume, complete with an elaborate headdress. I posed her against a background of perpendicular stripes, rather than a plain wall, so that there would be sufficient contrast to bring out her compelling facial bone structure." Hurrell played "All God's Chillun Got Rhythm" as she posed with an aura of mystery. She gave the impression that she had a dagger hidden in her sleeve.

Paulette Goddard. 1941.

Paulette Goddard

"I always looked forward to my sittings with Paulette Goddard," Hurrell comments, "because she was as fresh as a schoolgirl, both in looks and attitude. She was fond of big hats which framed her 'sweetheart' face. She never played the great star, even if she was dressed in furs and jewels for a fashion layout. She took the business of making pictures in stride. She could take direction expertly and gave exactly what was wanted. I always shot the dramatic stuff first, with soft music, then turned on a hot swing number or boogie woogie, and her mood changed instantly. I did impersonations, stood on my head, and acted the complete fool, and she loved it. She would laugh, her eyes would sparkle, and I'd press the bulb in my hand."

Mary Martin

Mary Martin tried her luck valiantly in films, but her infectious musical comedy personality, so effective over the footlights, never transferred successfully to the screen. Her first major film was *The Great Victor Herbert* in 1939. Although she would make ten other pictures, she never really hit her stride.

"She was not very photogenic, for one thing," recalls Hurrell, "and a full-face angle was best. She looked entirely different in profile. The Paramount makeup people had given her the 'treatment,' a new mouth, long false eyelashes and about a pound of makeup. I would have preferred to shoot her without the topping, with her face scrubbed clean.

"She was as down to earth as she could be in a white feather boa. She had a slight, but charming, Texas drawl. I played very romantic ballads and she became dreamy-eyed. I played down her prominent jaw by bringing the feathers up close to her face and uncovering her shoulders."

She met Richard Halliday, whom she later married, while she was at Paramount. Their marriage lasted until his death in 1971.

Unfortunately she was not allowed to film her two great stage musical roles, *South Pacific* and *The Sound of Music*.

Mary Martin before filming Happy Go Lucky. *1941.*

SAMUEL GOLDWYN

Samuel Goldwyn's studio on Santa Monica Boulevard in Hollywood was small and compact, with Spanish-style offices; its main gate was located on Formosa Avenue. Goldwyn released his pictures through United Artists and later through RKO. He was not afraid to spend money on films and also bought the best properties, writers, directors, and actors. Stars with whom he had or would have commitments or contracts were Merle Oberon, Gary Cooper, Ruth Chatterton, Walter Huston, Laurence Olivier, Danny Kaye, Eddie Cantor, Miriam Hopkins, Bette Davis, Herbert Marshall, Barbara Stanwyck, Dana Andrews, Ethel Merman, Fredric March, Farley Granger, Myrna Loy, and Virginia Mayo.

Samuel Goldwyn in his office. 1938.

Anna Sten

"I got this new gull," Samuel Goldwyn told Hurrell on the phone in 1934, "Name of Anyushka Stenski, we name her Anna Sten. She's going to be a big star. Come out. See what you can do. I want something special."

"She was in her late twenties," Hurrell recalls, "and inclined to be plump, although her figure was all right. She had rather nice eyes and nicely formed, natural teeth—not the usual Hollywood cap job. But outside of that, she was rather ordinary looking. Her Russian accent was quite charming and easily understood.

"When I looked through the lens, I found that her face could be entirely changed by lighting. Lights from different directions painted different pictures on her features. Her face was like a canvas. She wanted to be posed with two beautiful white Samoyeds. But although she was coop-

Anna Sten with the white Samoyeds in We Live Again. *1934.*

erative and lovely, the sled dogs were not. They continually yipped and yapped and, when not barking, menacingly bared their teeth. Finally, they quieted down long enough for me to get a few shots. I worked the entire day, and Sten changed clothing and coiffures several times.

"For months after the first Sten sitting, Goldwyn called me back to the studio. 'We shoot Anna today,' he would say. I took hundreds of exposures of her in costume, out of costume, and in street clothes. Each time Goldwyn would say, 'We make Anna a star.'" But no matter how often Hurrell photographed her, or how often her pictures appeared in the fan magazines and the rotogravure sections of newspapers, Anna Sten remained relatively unknown. Her two pictures in 1934, *Nana* and *We Live Again*; and *The Wedding Night* in 1935 were not successes. "Samuel Goldwyn spent a fortune promoting Anyushka Stenski into stardom," Hurrell says sadly, "only the public was not buying."

Gary Cooper in The Pride of
the Yankees. *1942.*

Gary Cooper. 1937.

Gary Cooper

Gary Cooper's ninety-odd-film career lasted from 1925 until his death in 1961 at the age of sixty. He was one of the first "personality" actors. "He never had any illusions about his ability as a star," Hurrell comments. "He took his work with a kind of bemused objectivity, although he was extremely professional. I think that only those people who worked with Coop really knew what a good actor he was, because he made everything look so effortless. He wasn't the nervous, high-powered sort of man that audiences grew tired of. He was always the hero; he couldn't play the heavy.

"I shot him many times from about 1934 to 1941. He was always on time and never missed an appointment. He wore no makeup for his gallery or studio sittings. Occasionally, when I photographed him on the set, he was somewhat condescending, but jovial and friendly. He seemed always to be saying: 'I'm here because my job demands it, so let's get on with it.' He put himself into my hands. He never demanded a mirror to check his face between shots or asked to see the proofs. When we were finished, he always came up to me and held out his hand. He didn't rush out of the gallery without saying good-bye. I liked best the shots where I was able to bring out his sly, sardonic quality."

Sigrid Gurie

Sigrid Gurie specialized in exotic parts. She had made both *The Adventures of Marco Polo*, with Gary Cooper and Basil Rathbone, and *Algiers*, with Charles Boyer and Hedy Lamarr in 1938.

"Sigrid Gurie," Hurrell says, "was married to a test pilot, and I was invited up to their house in Beverly Hills to shoot the pictures. I was greeted at the door, not by Miss Gurie, not by the aviator husband, but an ocelot with a very deep, growling voice. We glared at each other for a couple of seconds, then I heard a soft voice say, 'Stand very still.' I did as I was told, and Miss Gurie picked up the animal and took it to another room. We set up the equipment in the bar.

"Gurie changed into a flowing dress, and I found her very beautiful. Her skin glowed from being freshly scrubbed. I decided to play up her almond eyes. I adjusted my lights, thinking about what poses would be best, when she left the room for a second, then came back with the ocelot, which she placed on the bar. 'I must have some pictures with him,' she said, as he emitted a low, rumbling sound. 'Now, just stand very still. Be quiet and make no sudden moves, and everything will be all right!'

"My style was considerably cramped. Here I was with no music and with an animal that might turn vicious! I couldn't really pose the beast, so I lined him up in the camera, then said: 'Miss Gurie, just move in gingerly to the left side of his head.' Moving very slowly and feeling very frustrated, I took several films. She thanked me, removed the cat, and I was on my way. As it turned out, the beast was more photogenic than the beauty!"

Ronald Colman

Along with James Cagney, Edward G. Robinson, and Cary Grant, Ronald Colman was one of the most imitated actors in Hollywood. While his cultured English voice was easily impersonated, he did not find these impressions very amusing. Born in Surrey, England, in 1891, he came to the United States in 1920 and after a few mediocre films was chosen by Lillian Gish as her leading man in *The White Sister* (1923). His career would continue for thirty-seven years.

Hurrell reminisces: "Colman played best characters who were some-

what philosophical. Some of this intense introspection was held over in his portrait sittings. Like most European actors, he had a natural reserve. He was charming in an aloof way and, like Gary Cooper, somewhat condescending. Although he had perfect teeth, he did not like to expose them. His withdrawn manner rather intimidated me, so I played very loud, fast music to keep my own shooting tempo from faltering. At forty-six, Colman seemed young in appearance, but older in manner. I liked him better in formal dress than in tweeds."

Barbara Stanwyck

Barbara Stanwyck, née Ruby Stevens, was born July 16, 1907, in Brooklyn, New York. She started out as a chorus dancer in New York, then scored successes in two Broadway shows, *The Noose* and *Burlesque*. After her film debut in *Broadway Nights* for First National in 1927, she would make some eighty films, playing a wide variety of roles. She had no scruples about age: in 1932, at the age of twenty-five, she played Selina Peake in Edna Ferber's *So Big*, aging from a lovely young girl to a middle-aged woman. She would perform an even greater feat in *The Great Man's Lady*, ten years later, when she aged to 102. She played heroines and villainesses, straight dramatic roles (*The Bitter Tea of General Yen*, 1933), floozies (*Stella Dallas*, 1937), burlesque queens (*Ball of Fire*, 1942), western leads (*Annie Oakley*, 1935), and predatory females (*Double Indemnity*, 1944). She even played a lesbian madame (*A Walk on the Wild Side*, 1962), and was the courageous mother of three strapping boys in the television series *Big Valley* in the late 1960s and early 1970s.

"Although I photographed her often," Hurrell relates, "the shot that I like best was taken at the Sunset Boulevard studio. She wore no makeup at all, except a little lipstick, and her dark hair was drawn back from her face. I played romantic music that went with her rather ethereal mood that day. The prints, I felt, captured a facet of Barbara's personality that the fans didn't often see. Much later, I shot Gary Cooper, Theresa Wright, and her on the *Ball of Fire* set at Goldwyn. This time, in full makeup, it was a joy to show her spectacular legs in a revealing costume for the picture. She was an actress who could give you exactly what you wanted at the drop of a hat. My antics for her were very subdued."

OVERLEAF: *Barbara Stanwyck without makeup. 1938.*

Barbara Stanwyck as Sugarpuss O'Shea and Gary Cooper as Professor Bertram Potts in Ball of Fire. *1942.*

TWENTIETH CENTURY-FOX

The gallery at Twentieth Century-Fox, where Hurrell worked often on a free-lance basis, was luxurious. Cleverly designed, the place was 40 feet square and 20 feet high, which allowed for elaborate rigging, similar to the loft facilities provided by a legitimate theater. There was a large selection of "drops" and curtains, and one black-velvet drape that could be pulled into use at a moment's notice. There were also rolls of different colored paper to be rolled down if plain backgrounds were necessary. Props of all kinds were either on hand or easily acquired.

Twentieth Century Pictures had been formed by Darryl F. Zanuck, William Goetz, and Joseph M. Schenck in 1933, after Zanuck, who had been head of production at Warner Bros., left that company after a dispute about salary cuts inaugurated because of the depression. Zanuck was a brilliant, hard-driving man with a distinctive creative touch. Following a merger with Fox Film Corp., the new name, Twentieth Century-Fox came into being on August 15, 1934. Stars under contract were George Arliss, Shirley Temple, Tyrone Power, Alice Faye, Betty Grable, Loretta Young, Don Ameche, John Payne.

Shirley Temple

"Shirley Temple," Hurrell recalls, "had the photographic sense of someone four times her age. When I first shot her, she was seven years old, although the studio always put out that she was younger. We got along very well, fortunately—because she would only pose for photographers that she liked. Many of my confreres conducted a sitting as if it were High Mass, but because of my 'shows,' Shirley was always amused. She

Shirley Temple. 1939.

carried on quite professionally, although she must have been tired all the time because of her hectic schedules. I remember one time she fell asleep while I was changing a background. I shot her before she awakened. I would tap-dance, sing, and act a fool. Her mother, of course, was always present, whether the sitting took place at Twentieth or at my studio. Shirley was often sharply disciplined. I tried to intervene once—and only once, because Mrs. Temple snapped, 'Tend to your photography, Mr. Hurrell, and I'll attend to my daughter!'

"I continued to shoot Shirley quite often during the next few years and when she made *Kathleen* in 1941, which was her first 'grownup' role, I got a *Life* magazine assignment to do a cover and layout on her."

Shirley Temple. 1937.

Bill "Bojangles" Robinson.

Shirley Temple poses for her first glamour portrait at the age of thirteen for a Life magazine cover and layout.

Bill "Bojangles" Robinson

Bill "Bojangles" Robinson, the crackerjack tap-dancer, was brought to Twentieth Century-Fox for *The Little Colonel* in 1935, starring Shirley Temple. There was a kind of magic between the tall slim black man and the moppet with the golden curls. Robinson made two other pictures with her, *The Littlest Rebel* (1935), and *Rebecca of Sunnybrook Farm* (1938). The script writers always worked in a dance for them somewhere in the script, and Bojangles was always charming and believable in his role.

Hurrell says: "Sometimes I was called upon to do an 'obligatory' shot, as with the Robinson sitting. There was no other way that I could shoot Bojangles except doing his famous dance on the stairs—which he brought with him, all folded up. He was a bright, cheerful man, with polished mahogany skin.

"As all male dancers do before going 'on,' he emptied his pockets. In glancing over to the couch where he'd thrown his coins and keys, I was confounded to see a small thirty-eight revolver! He saw my shocked expression and told me that he had a license for the hand gun. He'd been involved in an altercation on Hollywood Boulevard some time before, when he'd been accosted by some hoodlums. The racial thing at that time was far different from what it is today, and he felt that he had to have some basic protection.

"I backlighted him strongly and went into kind of a caricature of the dance he was performing. I told him, 'Just dance for me, don't hold a stationary pose—and I'll get it!' I did, and when he saw the proofs, he pumped my hand and exclaimed: 'Man, that's *dignity!*' "

Dolores del Rio

"I photographed Dolores del Rio several times, sometimes on the set but more often at my studio. She was beautiful, with a flexible, mature kind of face. She would give me the exact expression that I wanted without a lot of coaxing. I played Mexican songs for her. Like Ramon Novarro, she was very proud of her heritage and spoke with affection of her country."

She was born Lolita Dolores Asunsolo de Martinez in Durango, Mexico, in 1905. Her first American film was *Joanna*, in 1925. She made the transition from silent films to talkies without any difficulty, and her exotic type of beauty was much in demand. She wore clothes extremely well and had a fashion-model figure. She continued, throughout the years, to make both American and Spanish pictures and did stage work in the United States and South America.

"She had the type of face," Hurrell continues, "that aged well. Her cheekbones were especially high so that her face could be lighted easily. I enjoyed working with her because she was so sincere and so eager to please."

Dolores del Rio. 1938.

Dolores del Rio poses on the moderne *staircase in her home. 1936.*

Sonja Henie

Sonja Henie came to Hollywood laden with medals. She had started to skate in 1921 at the age of eight and from 1927 to 1937 was World Champion ice-skater. Zanuck starred her in her first film, *One in a Million*, in 1936. Her films were so successful that she eventually made $160,000 per picture. An excellent businesswoman, she made investments in jewelry, art, and real estate.

"Sonja had a certain dimpled, naïve sweetness in front of the camera that I liked very much," recalls Hurrell. "What appeared to be chubbiness turned out to be all muscle from her years of skating. She was best from a front view, and her face was entirely different in repose. That first time, Twentieth Century-Fox gave her a glamorous makeup and a soft, feminine hairdo, and she was very upset when she discovered I knew it was a wig. Her costumes were always very elaborate—in fact, more and more elaborate as time went on. She came into the gallery without her skates, thinking that I would be taking only head and shoulders. But she looked so fresh and wholesome that I asked her to lean against a table while I took a full-length shot of her.

"I photographed her several times at her home, where she posed either in the living room or outside in the garden. She was most gracious, always bubbling over with energy. She had exactly the sort of moneyed life that she'd always imagined. She meant to have a good time. My favorite shot of her was not in the ruffles and furbelows that she wore in her skating pictures, but a quiet, subdued shot that I took one day at her house. She'd just come in from I. Magnin's, and I said, 'Let's take a couple right now.' The prints showed a poised, pensive Sonja Henie."

Annabella

"Annabella had dramatic flair," relates Hurrell. "She wasn't the least bit kittenish."

Annabella, whose real name was Suzanne Carpentier, made her English-speaking debut in *Wings of the Morning* in 1937, and for the next ten years appeared in both American and French film productions. She starred in *Suez* in 1938 with Loretta Young and Tyrone Power—whom she subsequently married.

Hurrell recalls, "Annabella's shoulders were especially good. I gave her a white fur to hug around her bosom when I made the shots. Zanuck was pleased with the results, as he envisioned her as a glamour personality. But although she certainly was appealing, she never became a sexpot."

ABOVE LEFT: *Sonja Henie at her home.* 1938.

ABOVE: *Annabella.* 1938.

Gypsy Rose Lee

"Gypsy Rose Lee was known as Louise Hovick when I photographed her," Hurrell states. "Zanuck had brought her out from New York, and it was thought that because of her background in burlesque, she would become the next big sex symbol. She was only twenty-four, but she had a bold, strong, mature kind of beauty and sophistication, and a hard veneer. I guess it was because she'd been in show business since the age of six.

"She could turn on the dramatics at the drop of a handkerchief. She had a full, round face and beautiful body, which she refused to accentuate. She was conscious of an uneven front tooth and would not laugh for me. She wore street clothes for the sitting; hat, gloves, and furs. I angled my boom light to light her face from the left, to play down the fullness of her face. The prints turned out very well, but I still wish I could have photographed her in a negligee."

Gypsy Rose Lee. 1937.

Loretta Young & Tyrone Power

"Loretta Young," says Hurrell, smiling, "was one of the most inventive subjects that I ever shot. She always had exciting ideas about the way that she should be photographed. She had *radiance*. I don't believe that we ever, during the next twenty-five years that we worked together, repeated a pose. She was a disciplined pro, having made her first picture, *Naughty But Nice,* for Mervyn LeRoy in 1927 when she was only fifteen. When I shot her during her television anthology show, which lasted from 1953 to 1961, she was just as bright and clever and just as cooperative. She is still just as radiant today!"

"Ty Power," Hurrell smiles, "was handsome and quite easy to shoot. But a certain depth in his eyes that came through in his photographs said more about him than anything else. Ty was quiet and gentlemanly, lithe and graceful, he posed willingly, without complaint." Power performed his duty in a collection of vapid, leading-man roles in the 1930s, but did not come into his own until the forties, especially with W. Somerset Maugham's *The Razor's Edge* in 1946 and *Nightmare Alley* in 1947.

"The day that I shot Loretta Young and him, I wanted to create a special feeling beyond the usual clinch. When I asked Loretta, who was wearing a terry-cloth bathrobe, to lift her chin and saw that great swan neck, I moved Power in behind her. I asked her to lower the material around her shoulders, then I lighted her face from the front, while Ty made up the background. It was one of the most unusual compositions that I ever made."

Loretta Young and Tyrone Power. 1937. (Jacket photograph)

SELZNICK INTERNATIONAL

Selznick International Pictures was founded by David O. Selznick in 1936, and quickly became a force in the industry. Selznick had gained wide experience in the business, first as an assistant to his father who ran a film exchange in New York, and then later as a producer at RKO and M.G.M. Money was never an object where a Selznick picture was concerned. David O. contracted for the best screen properties, the most prestigious stars, the most brilliant cinematographers, and the most knowledgeable technicians. He placed many stars under long-term contract, and then when no pictures were scheduled, he loaned them to other studios for tremendous sums—while still paying them low contract rates. His stable of players included Janet Gaynor, Fredric March, Ronald Colman, Ingrid Bergman, Jennifer Jones, Joseph Cotten, Joan Fontaine and many others, some of whom never made a Selznick International picture but were loaned to other companies. Like Samuel Goldwyn, David O. Selznick appreciated Hurrell's work and often used his services, both on the set and at the Sunset Boulevard studio.

Janet Gaynor

Gaynor won the first Academy Award in the 1927–28 period for three films: *Seventh Heaven, Sunrise,* and *Street Angel.* She was the ultimate gamine, the appealing waif. She and Charles Farrell were a famous screen team from 1927 to 1934; they made twelve memorable films together. She made the original version of *A Star Is Born* (1937), with Fredric March. She came out of retirement in 1957 to do *Bernadine.*

"When I was asked finally to photograph Janet Gaynor," Hurrell relates, "she was making what turned out to be her last starring picture, *The Young in Heart,* produced by David O. Selznick. She was a charmer, winsome and unprepossessing; I'd not realized from seeing her on the screen that she was so tiny. I gave her a white gardenia to relieve the bleakness of her black costume. I would've liked to have shot her in color because her reddish hair was extremely photogenic, and her slightly freckled complexion was smooth and creamy. We got along very well. I remember I played rumba music—which was all the rage—and she was enthusiastic all during the sitting."

OPPOSITE: *Janet Gaynor in* The Young in Heart. *1938.*

Fredric March as Norman Maine in A Star Is Born. *1937.*

Fredric March

Fredric March was thirty-two when he made his first major film in 1929; it was *The Dummy*, starring Ruth Chatterton. He was debonair and handsome, but not conceited; he would play parts that no other good-looking actor would consider. Other than Paul Muni, he was the first leading-man type to play character roles. His 1932 film *Dr. Jekyll and Mr. Hyde* (which won him an Academy Award) awakened producers to his abilities. *Death Takes a Holiday*, 1934, in which he played death, was a departure, as was his Jean Valjean in *Les Misérables* in 1934, and the title role in *Anthony Adverse* in 1936. In 1941 he played a minister in *One Foot in Heaven*; in 1942, a warlock in *I Married a Witch*; in 1944, Samuel Clemens (in a remarkable makeup created by Perc Westmore) in *The Adventures of Mark Twain;* and in 1946 he won a second Academy Award in *The Best Years of Our Lives.*

Hurrell says: "March was quiet, serious, and very sober-faced. He posed for photographs as a necessary part of his regimen, but I could not say he was an ideal subject. It was very difficult to get him to laugh. Perhaps he regarded himself as too dedicated an actor to put up with a lot of tomfoolery; although he was certainly pleasant enough off-camera. I would jump around a bit, but I'm afraid he did not find me very entertaining. He did his job and I did mine, and that was that!"

Hedy Lamarr

"Although Hedy Lamarr did not have the strong bone structure of a Garbo, her beauty was so outstanding that any angle was good. I did try, however, to make her cheeks look less full. She wasn't always in a sultry mood, so it was necessary to build an atmosphere of excitement around her, which I usually accomplished with music. The first time I shot her was at her house in 1938, just after she had finished her first picture, *Algiers*, with Charles Boyer. She was quiet and introspective, and I set up my camera equipment very quickly to catch the mood before it faded. Her coloring, smooth white skin, and raven black hair were so spectacular I wished I had brought along some color film. I didn't use any of my usual tricks. I realized instantly that she was one of those actresses who can wear an absolutly blank expression and yet convey an attitude of complete intrigue. They can sometimes be more expressive before the still camera than on the motion picture set."

ℳadeleine 𝒞arroll

The Prisoner of Zenda sets at Selznick International in 1937 were magnificent specimens of the art director's domain. Hurrell went to an interior castle set to photograph Madeleine Carroll in modern dress for publicity pictures.

"Madeleine Carroll," he recalls with a smile, "was one of the most beautiful women in Hollywood at that time. Her blond, spun-gold hair, generous mouth, and large, expressive eyes were extremely photogenic. She had a natural grace, and was very relaxed before the camera. Her face was rather full, and showed up best straight into the camera rather than a profile or three-quarters shot. She was not temperamental or fiery; in fact, she was rather introverted. She responded extremely well to Latin music, which I played incessantly for her sittings."

Warner Bros.

Robert Taplinger, in publicity at Warner Bros. in Burbank, occasionally dropped by the Sunset studio during the last months of 1938. He implied at first, and then finally stated, that the valley studio would be most interested in placing Hurrell under contract. "He finally wore me down," Hurrell laughs. "He always pointed out that I would be free of responsibility, no books to keep, and no rent to pay. As time went on, of course, the pot got sweeter and sweeter. I hemmed and hawed until he made an offer that I couldn't refuse—a thousand dollars a week for a two-year contract—as head portrait photographer. This stipend wouldn't interfere with my commercial activities, including my Lux Soap account, which paid fifteen hundred dollars per star photograph. I still had my monthly page in *Esquire* also, plus other lesser assignments."

In August of 1938, Hurrell closed the Sunset Boulevard facility and St. Hilaire and he traveled over the hills to Burbank. Warner Bros. was an exceptionally progressive plant. In the mid-1920s the four Warner brothers (Sam, Harry, Albert, and Jack) had pioneered sound pictures when no other studio in town was interested. They had set Hollywood on its ear in 1927 with *The Jazz Singer*, the first feature film to combine musical numbers with dialogue. From the immense popularity of those first "talkies," they had purchased the new First National Studios in Burbank in 1929 for ten million dollars in cash.

Warner Bros. started the gangster cycle with *Doorway to Hell* and *Little Caesar* in 1930, rejuvenated musical comedies with *42nd Street* in 1933 and were responsible for hundreds of socially conscious pictures taken from newspaper headlines, and biography pictures like *The Life of Emile Zola* that were successful examples of fine production. Among the stars under contract were Bette Davis, James Cagney, Edward G. Robinson, Ann Sheridan, Ida Lupino, John Garfield, Errol Flynn, Humphrey Bogart, Paul Muni, Leslie Howard, and Olivia de Havilland.

Elmer Fryer, who had been in charge of the portrait department, was moved next door, and Hurrell was given the large gallery, which was the most modern facility in town. A balcony had been installed for storage of lamps and other paraphernalia, and more equipment was available than would ever be needed. One end of the gallery featured huge doors so that scenery and props could be delivered via truck. When Hurrell required background working materials, he stopped by the Property Department and made his selection from hundreds of divans, chairs, bric-a-brac, and paintings. He was also presented with a cabinet phonograph with large separate speakers and crates of new records. He attached a thirty-foot hose to the shutter of his camera so he could move about the gallery with ease. In short, he was given carte blanche.

Edward G. Robinson

Edward G. Robinson. 1938.

One of the most dedicated actors on the lot was Edward G. Robinson. He did not have great physical stature; he was not good-looking in the conventional sense; and he was not a great lover boy, but he had charisma and a huge box-office following. Born Emmanuel Goldenberg in Bucharest, Rumania in 1893, he emigrated to the United States as a boy, and later worked as an actor and playwright. He made his film debut in *The Bright Shawl,* in 1923, but *Little Caesar* in 1931 established him as a gangster, a part he would play off and on throughout his career—sometimes seriously and sometimes comically. He was essentially a character actor par excellence.

"Eddie would treat a sitting as a big production," Hurrell recalls. "He'd come in with several suits, shirts, neckties, hats, gloves, scarves, and a box of cigars. We'd smoke while he was changing. He had great enthusiasm and would stay all day if necessary. He'd run through his bag of tricks, cigar stuck in the side of his mouth, that 'I've swallowed the whole world' smile, and that famous stance, feet planted firmly apart, hands behind his back. When he'd given me the whole works, then he'd say: 'Okay, okay, what'll we do next?' And we'd do a few straight poses. While he was getting his gear together, he'd lapse into his offscreen character, mild, amusing, and unassuming, and tell me about a new painting he had just bought, or a visit to a museum he'd just made with his wife. But when I think about Eddie now, I see him still with his cigar jutting out in a jaunty fashion, his eyes wide and boring, a revolver faintly outlined under his coat—the Big Eddie that I knew so well."

Paul Muni

"Shadrach, Meshach, Abednego," Hurrell sang at the top of his lungs. Paul Muni, seated sedately on a chair, surrounded by lights, smiled crookedly, and Hurrell pressed the bulb.

"Mr. Muni had the same problem relaxing before a still camera that his European buddies had," comments Hurrell. "He just couldn't let go. In the first place, he didn't like to be photographed. I guess he was so used to the wigs, beards, and padding used in his films that he felt naked sans makeup. Actually, he was a handsome man, with strong features and very expressive eyes. He'd built his reputation on a handful of films, but was still billed as *Mr.* Paul Muni, a rarity in Hollywood."

After the session, Hurrell received a call from Bella, Muni's rather aggressive wife, calling from home. "The pictures are *so* good, I like them very much." She lowered her voice, "And, by the way, so does Muni."

Paul Muni. 1938.

Bette Davis

Bette Davis was the undisputed queen of the lot. Bob Hope once introduced her at a Hollywood function as the "fourth Warner Brother." She had been with the studio since 1932, but it was not until *Of Human Bondage* at RKO in 1934 that she was given a role that showed off her dramatic talent. When her name did not appear on the Academy nominations ballot, a write-in vote was accepted for the first time. She won her first Oscar for *Dangerous* in 1935 and her second for *Jezebel* in 1938. During her career, she was nominated ten times for an Academy Award.

"During the two years that I was at Warner Bros., I photographed Bette more than any other star," recalls Hurrell. "Our personal rapport was uncanny. I remember especially when she came into the gallery for the *Dark Victory* sitting, there was something in her face that I'd not seen before. I'd always considered her attractive, but now she had a special kind of beauty. I played classical music, which I didn't do often for her, because we both liked upbeat tunes. When I looked through the lens, there was a compelling force about her, a kind of inner anguish that could only mean she was going through a difficult time personally. She never alluded to it, and neither did I, but the camera never lies. The portraits I took of Judith Traherne, the brave gal who has only six months to live, were the most extraordinary shots I ever took of Bette.

"By the time I shot her for *Juarez* and *The Old Maid*, she was back to her old self, fun-loving, amusing, and always enthusiastic. I'd go into impossible routines and she'd laugh until her mascara ran. She had another extraordinary quality—that Lombard also had—the ability to switch from a gay, laughing pose to a completely dramatic attitude in a matter of seconds.

"Later, when she was making *The Little Foxes* at Goldwyn, she personally asked for me to shoot portraits of Regina Giddens. She was playing a much older role. I made her look more mature by harsh lighting. With her hair in a pompadour, white makeup, her tiny figure corseted in Gibson Girl attire, she was every inch the older version of a Southern belle."

Bette Davis as Judith Traherne in Dark Victory. *She considers this shot one of the most revealing ever taken of her. 1939.*

OPPOSITE: *Bette Davis poses for a glamour shot for* You *magazine to show a new hairstyle. 1938.*

LEFT: *Bette Davis as Leslie Crosbie in W. Somerset Maugham's* The Letter. *1940.*

RIGHT: *Bette Davis as Regina Giddens in* The Little Foxes. *1941.*

The Private Lives of Elizabeth and Essex

The Private Lives of Elizabeth and Essex was to be photographed in Technicolor to record the pageantry and pomp and circumstance of the Court of Elizabeth I. A long series of sittings was booked with Hurrell, not only in the still gallery, but on the sets. Einfield, head of exploitation, wanted the widest coverage possible. No expense was to be spared. The most daring aspect of the production was the casting of Bette Davis as Elizabeth.

"Bette was the only top actress in Hollywood at that time," Hurrell relates, "who would have appeared to such physical disadvantage. She jumped on the role because it gave her a chance to show a different facet of her talent. Her hairline and eyebrows were shaved. A pasty makeup was devised that would appear flat and unflattering in the camera, and she also wore a series of bright red wigs, so placed as to give the illusion of baldness. Her costumes, designed by Orry-Kelly, were authentic. In fact, the whole production was authentic. When I shot her, I threw away all of the usual tricks. Out for character development, I shot her harshly to make her look sixty, which was not easy as she was about thirty at the time, and naturally good-looking. From the proof stage, the negs went straight to the printing department, the only time I can recall from my stay at Warners that no retouching was employed.

"I went into my usual comedy routines to keep the atmosphere from becoming static. Played modern music and old time stuff. She and I had a wonderful rapport, since I photographed her so often, but on *Elizabeth and Essex*, we both tried especially hard to bring out a depth of character in the queen. As the picture wore on and on, Bette got thinner and thinner: the physical demands of the role were hard on her, plus the weight of all those heavy costumes. By the time we finished shooting, I don't think she could have weighed more than eighty-five or ninety pounds.

"Errol Flynn, as Essex, was his usual devil-may-care self. In order to get character in his shots, I relied mostly on lighting.

"I was on the set one day, my lights set up, ready to shoot as soon as the principals arrived from makeup and wardrobe, when Jack L. Warner arrived, wearing a hat and with the collar of his suit turned up—the way

Bette Davis as Queen Elizabeth. 1939.

he usually toured the sets. I was joking with a gaffer when I heard him say, 'Well, what are *you* doing?' I replied, 'Waiting to take some shots, Mr. Warner.' By this time more people were assembled on the set, and seeing he had an audience, his voice grew louder. 'Well, I'm not paying you a thousand bucks a week to stand around talking. Why don't you get busy?' He turned on his heel, leaving me red and mumbling. Then he began to laugh. I had seen him pull this same stunt on others before, but it was the first time he gave me this routine, and the last."

ABOVE LEFT: *Olivia de Havilland as Lady Penelope Gray in* The Private Lives of Elizabeth and Essex. *1939.*

ABOVE: *Errol Flynn in* The Private Lives of Elizabeth and Essex. *1939.*

Errol Flynn.

Errol Flynn

Errol Flynn was unique in the Warner Bros. lineup of stars in that he was not put through a long succession of "B" pictures as a training ground. Even Cagney and Robinson toiled for years in the concrete jungles of cheap hood roles before reaching respectable box-office status. Flynn enjoyed a decent fan following almost from the beginning of his career.

He also had an exceptional background, far more exotic than any role he ever played. Few contemporaries really believed that he was born in Hobart on the Island of Tasmania. But Flynn was a true, devil-may-care adventurer before the age of twenty-five. He had, at one time or another, panned for gold, worked for passage on a variety of ships, grown tobacco, castrated sheep with his teeth, hunted tropical birds, smuggled jewels, served with the New Guinea constabulary, and even portrayed Fletcher Christian in an Australian film, *In the Wake of the Bounty*, before appearing in his first film in England, *Murder in Monte Carlo*.

Flynn's charm was a combination of tenderness, fierce aggressiveness, and ingenuity. Women responded to his virile, devastating sexuality and fantasized about being in his arms. Men identified with the fearless satyr who fought his enemies with superhuman ingenuity and a slightly mocking expression. He won enormous audiences throughout the world. He was the personification of the ultimate hero in both straight and swashbuckling roles. His films were phenomenally successful. But Flynn actually felt he was cursed by his good looks.

Flynn and Hurrell enjoyed an easy relationship. One day, Flynn arrived for his sitting followed by a wardrobe man with an armload of suits, ties, and sweaters. Since Ann Sheridan had just departed, Hurrell left the same rumba record on the phonograph. He made the shots, then Flynn began to pick over the garments. "Let's see, a paisley tie would be smashing with this tweed, don't you think? But maybe a sweater would look more casual."

"In 1939 he was thirty years old and easy to photograph, but only a few years later, after a hard night, he would show up with huge 'balloon tires' under his eyes. I was glad that I didn't photograph him during his last years when drink had played havoc with his face. When he died, at fifty, the autopsy showed he was physically a man of seventy-five."

Humphrey Bogart

Bogart was a seasoned performer on the stage before he made his first Hollywood pictures in 1930. It took six years before he caught the imagination of the public as the pathological holdup man, Duke Mantee, in *The Petrified Forest*. He went on to play an assortment of gangsters, killers, confidence men, and other misunderstood types. It was *The Maltese Falcon*, in 1942, in which he played Sam Spade, that was his real departure from supporting roles in big star productions and leads in "B"-grade films. After *Casablanca* two years later, he was firmly entrenched as the cynical, disillusioned man whom the fates had suspended in a kind of purgatory. In 1951 when he won an Academy Award for *The African Queen*, playing a rum-pot "brother" of Sam Spade, it seemed at last that he had brought his basic screen character into sharp and lasting focus.

"Among the actors at Warners," reveals Hurrell, "Bogie was positively unique. If Gable and I were comrades, Bogie and I were conspirators. He was very serious about his work, which a lot of people never realized. He would strike poses that were familiar to him, the upward look, hand rubbing jaw, the business with a cigarette, then he'd say: 'Okay, kid let's do something different,' and we'd maneuver new positions and new expressions. The music was always loud and furious.

"He was not the easiest man to photograph, and he knew it. 'Leave in the lines,' he would say, 'I'm proud of 'em.' In earlier photographs his famous lip scar was retouched, but it had become so famous by the time I reached Warners that we pretty much left it alone. It became his trademark. The scar had been caused shortly after World War I, when Bogart was escorting military prisoners, and was hit in the mouth by a handcuffed prisoner.

"He was a notorious 'needler,' but he never needled me. He was too professional to engage in this sort of pastime when working. Later on, he began to lose his hair and wore a rather good rug. 'I never appear professionally without it,' he told me, 'because that guy up there on the screen has a full head of hair.' "

Humphrey Bogart.

Frank Capra

"Frank Capra was one of those hot-shot, take-charge, hard driving, creative guys who never let down," says Hurrell, "and he'd made a lot of important films at Columbia.

"I shot Capra in profile, looking off into the distance. When I examined the proofs, I decided to touch up his receding hairline. When he saw the results, he hollered, 'What in the hell did you do *that* for?' His famous Sicilian temper was on display. I took the negs and removed, hair by hair, all the fur that I had added, and he laughed and said, 'Now, that's me!' and okayed the pictures."

Frank Capra.

Elsa Maxwell in one of the great gag photographs of Hurrell's career.

Elsa Maxwell

"One of the most amusing shots I ever took came about quite by accident," Hurrell says, laughing. "Elsa Maxwell, who was a great friend of Jack and Ann Warner's, came in to do a fashion layout, featuring clothes for the 'plump' figure. Since Elsa weighed in the neighborhood of two hundred and fifty pounds, I knew, even before we started shooting, that I would have to trim away at least fifty pounds by retouching.

"Elsa was a jolly sort, always laughing and making jokes. Her lack of beauty was forgotten the moment she opened her mouth. Her conversation was laced with genuine wit. After we were finished with the fashion stuff, she spied the bear rug on the floor in the corner. 'I've got to try this, George. Watch me, I'll out-Harlow Harlow!' She waddled over to the rug and, with some difficulty, got down on her knees. She crawled up to the bear's head, straightened out her body, and posed. I said, 'Don't move, Elsa. I've got to get this shot!' And I did!"

James Cagney

From 1930 to 1942, when he left the studio, Cagney filmed forty-one pictures at Warner Bros. When he retired to his farm in Martha's Vineyard in 1961, he said, "I've had it." He never again stepped on a motion-picture lot.

"Every working day of his life," Hurrell comments, "Jimmy Cagney would report for work exactly on time, just as if he were going to a job at a bank or a department store. When he wasn't working, he never came on the lot. Then he was off relaxing with his wife, 'my Bill,' who had also been in vaudeville. I never saw him without heavy makeup. He had sandy hair and a pug nose, and he liked to change his eyebrows. He knew he was not a glamour-boy type. He handled a sitting just as professionally as he handled a character in a script. He would come into the gallery, sit down, strike a few attitudes, and I'd take a few shots. Then he'd bark, 'What now?' Since he was usually serious, I'd clown around to get that delightful twisted smile of his. Sometimes I'd really have to do a number. It was as if he knew what I wanted, but wanted to see how exhausted I could become before he would give it to me. All of his reaction came from inside. His eyes could bore a hole through you."

John Garfield

John Garfield made a tremendous impact in his first film, *Four Daughters*, in 1938. He was twenty-five years old at the time.

"He was a strange, fascinating guy," recalls Hurrell, "He couldn't sit still. There was a frantic air about him which I understood because of my own restless nature. Thank God I worked quickly, because I was able to catch him in a number of interesting attitudes. He lent *action* to his shots. He moved constantly and I pressed the bulb in my hand again and again. We created our own tempo. He never thought he was good looking. 'I'm a mug,' he would laugh, 'just a mug.' But occasionally, I'd get a beautiful shot of him that was flattering and yet had depth. He'd look at the proofs and say: 'Ain't too bad for a kid from the Bronx, eh?' and he'd roar with laughter."

James Cagney.

John Garfield. 1939.

Ann Sheridan. 1939.

$\mathcal{A}nn$ $\mathcal{S}heridan$

Ann Sheridan arrived in Hollywood after winning Paramount's 'Search for Beauty' contest in 1933. When Hurrell came to Warner Bros. she was having a career upturn, playing dramatic parts in *Angels with Dirty Faces* in 1938 and *They Made Me a Criminal* in 1939. Taplinger looked over the Warner Bros. stock company and decided that Sheridan's type should be changed. She was a tall and beautiful redhead with an exciting low, contralto voice. Walter Winchell coined the term "oomph" to typify sex appeal. Ann Sheridan was duly christened "The Oomph Girl"—a sobriquet supposedly voted upon by Lucius Beebe, Busby Berkeley, Earl Carroll, Bob Hope, Robert L. Ripley, and Earl of Warwick, and nineteen other ultrasophisticated men.

A huge publicity campaign was planned and she was booked into the gallery for an extensive series of sittings. "She was very good-natured about the whole thing," Hurrell remembers. "I played rumba and samba records and she was totally responsive. We laughed a good deal because the beauty mark, courtesy of Perc Westmore, kept sliding down her cheek from the heat of the lights. It was only later that she grew tired of the 'Oomph Girl' tag. 'What's Oomph?' she'd say. 'That's what a fat man says when he bends over to tie his shoelaces!' "

Gilbert Roland

"Gil Roland had an animal sexuality that leaped out at the camera," Hurrell recalls. "He had been a bullfighter in Mexico and the grace he'd learned in the ring gave him an easy manner. He was cheerful and especially responsive to music—any kind of music. Although he'd been around since the silent days, he was a dependable actor and had been very good with Mae West in *She Done Him Wrong* in 1933. While quite easy to pose, he was very critical of his photographs. He took a long time to go through a batch of proofs, because he paid special attention to his facial expression. I always shot many more plates than necessary to give him a wider selection. Today on a movie set, he still has that animal magnetism."

Randolph Scott

Randolph Scott was on the lot in 1940 to film *Virginia City* with Errol Flynn and Miriam Hopkins. He had started in 1931 with *Women Men Marry* for Headline Pictures. A tall, thin, rather aesthetic looking young man, he was cast in "early Gary Cooper"-type movies. Although he had appeared in melodramas (*Murders in the Zoo*, 1933), musicals (*Roberta*, 1935), dramas (*So Red the Rose*, 1935), and comedies (*My Favorite Wife*, 1940), his rather dry personality seemed especially right for the Western Hero, short on words and long on action. He had played opposite such diversified ladies as Irene Dunne, Helen Gahagan, and Shirley Temple.

"Randy," says Hurrell, "was an upper-crust guy, with a good education and background that many stars envied. It was always a source of amusement to me that this charming society-type lad was such a hit in Westerns. He came into the gallery in his costume for *Virginia City*, wearing his six-shooter. We tried a few poses, then I said: 'How about putting your foot up on that stool and drawing your gun?' He did so rather self-consciously. I said: 'Do it again, please.' Again. Again. He became so involved in drawing the pistol that he forgot about me. When we had finished, he grabbed my hand. 'Thank you, George,' he said, and he meant it. I was glad I had made the ordeal of posing a little easier for him."

Gilbert Roland. *1939*.

Randolph Scott in Virginia
City. *1940*.

Alexis Smith

Alexis Smith came to Warner Bros. in 1940 at the age of nineteen, after being discovered at Los Angeles City College. "She had a frosty kind of beauty," recalls Hurrell, "that photographed exceptionally well. That patrician type of beauty, like Norma Shearer and Irene Dunne, comes over very well in the camera. Alexis was tall and very graceful. I liked her as a subject, although she did not project much personality in repose. I used all sorts of tricks to make her forget who and where she was. I played boogie-woogie, with an occasional violin piece thrown in for good measure. One day she came in right from makeup with every curl in place. She was breathtakingly beautiful, but also as perfect as a statue. Since I was to shoot glamour stuff, the first thing I did was to ask her to run her fingers through her hair, then I gave her a long piece of gold-and-silver cloth to wrap around her shoulders. This shot of her slightly disheveled beauty was the best of the lot."

Alexis Smith. 1940.

Doris Duke

Doris Duke. 1940.

Taplinger told Hurrell that he could use the gallery on a weekend to photograph Doris Duke, who had called about a sitting. The appointment was arranged for a Saturday afternoon.

"I left her a pass at the gate," Hurrell relates, "and she and her housekeeper drove on the lot, and parked their old ramshackle car outside the gallery. She wore a very simple, nondescript dress and carried over her arm a gown she had just purchased. She was friendly, but rather sedate. No one could possibly tell from her appearance that she was a multimillionairess. However, she had the manner and the bearing of one born with wealth. After changing, she came into the gallery holding her dress in back with one hand. 'I'm afraid it doesn't fit,' she said. 'Don't worry about a thing,' I told her, 'we'll fix that in the posing.'

"She had a strange sort of allure, an unusual beauty, but her most striking feature was her almond eyes. I played loud jazz music and the sitting was over rather quickly. She changed and I walked her out to her car, still amused that the 'richest girl in the world' had posed for my camera with safety pins holding her dress in place."

The Waldorf and Rodeo Drive

During the last months of Hurrell's contract at Warner Bros., he was in a financial position to build his own studio. The site was finally selected: 333 Rodeo Drive in Beverly Hills. The construction of the new building was not yet completed when he left the Burbank studio. Since he was tired, and unusually restless, in the spring of 1941 he loaded up his Buick station wagon with equipment and gear, and drove across country to New York.

He took a short lease on a studio at the Waldorf Astoria Hotel. There Hurrell photographed a bevy of socialites, and completed some commercial jobs for advertising agencies. After being cooped up in a still gallery for two years, New York provided the fast-paced excitement that was much to his liking. He felt very much at home.

Helena Rubinstein

"I had seen opulence in my time," Hurrell recalls, "but not on the Rubinstein scale. I was flabbergasted at the fabulous collection of objets d'art and antiques in her large apartment. I was reminded of a million-dollar movie set.

"Madame Rubinstein was beautiful in the Old World sense, and although she was the world's leading exponent of cosmetics, she was very simply made up. Her profile was exquisite—like a European-cut cameo. Her gown and jewels were spectacular, and though dressed as elegantly as any queen, she didn't play the 'grande dame.' "

After closing the Waldorf studio, Hurrell headed for Beverly Hills.

He had been ensconced on Rodeo Drive only a few weeks when he heard a familiar voice calling from the reception room: " 'Alloo, M'ster 'urell!"

He looked up to find Garbo standing in the door. She was dressed in trousers, pullover, and slouch hat. She was more beautiful than he had remembered. Maturity had given her face a special glow. She was in excellent spirits.

"Thought I would come by and see how my new tenant is doing." Her blue eyes twinkled mischievously.

"*You* are my landlady?"

"Yes," she laughed. "It pleases me very much to have you on my property. Show me around, please."

Garbo quietly appraised each piece of equipment. Hurrell had never felt that she was especially aware of technical matters on the set. To him, her performance was always foremost. "But," he says, "she was very astute and completely knowledgeable. Before she left, I popped the old question, 'How about some shots?' 'Oh, no, no, M'ster 'urell. I am not photographed any more.' She waved and was gone."

Madame Helena Rubinstein. 1940.

Jane Russell

Publicist Russell Birdwell booked an appointment for Jane Russell, an unknown starlet who was finishing *The Outlaw* for Howard Hughes. Birdwell gave him a rundown on the Western script. Hurrell's mind began to whirl. Suddenly a series of pictures came into his mind's eye. "A haystack!" He exclaimed. "I'll shoot Jane Russell in a haystack!"

Birdwell was incredulous. "This isn't a location job," he said sourly.

"No. No. We won't go to the haystack, the haystack will come to us."

The next morning a feed and seed store in Santa Monica transferred half a ton of fresh-smelling hay to Rodeo Drive. It is doubtful if so bucolic a commodity had ever been delivered to such an exclusive area of expensive shops.

"Jane," Hurrell relates, "was twenty years old, and rather shy. Modeling jobs had given her a certain professional grace, and she took direction very well. Although striking in appearance, she did not seem to be conscious of her lush, fresh beauty or her ample physical endowments. She brought several skirts and low-cut blouses she'd worn in the picture. Much has been printed over the years about the famous Hughes-designed brassiere, but Jane Russell wore no such device that day.

"My shooting tempo was, as always, very fast. In three hours, I had exposed over fifty plates, in both color and black and white. I received fifteen hundred dollars for the job, and went on to my next sitting. I had no idea that the photographs, which were subsequently distributed all over the world, would be one of the causes of *The Outlaw*'s being banned. The picture was not released until two years later, by which time Jane Russell's name was known in every household.

"There were two catch phrases used in connection with the exploitation of the film, and they always broke me up when I looked at the shots: 'How would you like to tussle with Russell?' and 'What are the two great reasons for Jane Russell's rise to stardom?'"

OVERLEAF LEFT: The Outlaw. *1942.*

RIGHT: *Jane Russell. 1946.*

Gene Tierney

In *The Shanghai Gesture* in 1941, Gene Tierney was set to portray Poppy, the illegitimate Eurasian daughter of Ona Munson's Mother Goddam (changed by United Artists to "Mother Gin-Sling," because of the Production Code). Although she had appeared in five previous pictures, this was to be her first "dress-up" role.

"She arrived on Rodeo Drive with only one costume change, a gown that her husband, Oleg Cassini, had designed for the picture. I was very conscious of the presence of Cassini. Although he stayed politely in the background, I felt he was giving me silent instructions on exactly how she should be photographed. I played up her almond-shaped eyes, which gave her an exotic appearance. She was cooperative, and actually very sweet. She did not strike attitudes, but waited for instructions. Because of her round face, I created a hollow cheek effect by lighting. Later, I went to the studio and made a color shot of her posed with a statue for *Esquire* magazine, but by that time she was more camera-wise. I also felt more at home because Mr. Cassini was not lurking in the background."

Gene Tierney, for Esquire. *1944.*

Gene Tierney as Poppy in The Shanghai Gesture. *1941.*

Betty Grable

Betty Grable had made a long succession of pictures as a vivacious blonde dancer with an engaging laugh and a pleasant singing voice. But it was not until *Down Argentine Way* in 1940 that she began to acquire a fan following, and was on her way to the top ten box-office stars.

"*Esquire* asked me to take pinup shots, and a deal was made with Twentieth Century-Fox," Hurrell says. "It was a very cold day and the heating unit in the gallery had gone kaflooey. Betty arrived wrapped in a fur coat. She was bouncy and jolly, but cold. I asked her to do a few dance steps to warm her up. She tossed the coat on a chair and began to work out in her bathing suit. 'That sound you hear is my teeth chattering,' she laughed.

I worked very quickly, playing loud swing music. About twenty minutes later we finished. She blew me a kiss and said, 'That's for making the session so short,' then she wrapped the coat around her and ran out to her limousine. When I looked at the proofs through a magnifying glass, Betty Grable's magnificent gams were covered with goosebumps!"

Betty Grable. 1942.

Veronica Lake

"Paramount Publicity called early one morning in 1941 to ask if I could work with Veronica Lake during the late afternoon. She was on the lot

shooting *Sullivan's Travels*, and they needed the shots in a hurry. I made the appointment for five-thirty. At exactly five forty-five, a limousine drove up and Veronica, wearing hair curlers under a snood, came into the studio followed by a makeup man, a hairdresser, and a publicity man. She was very tired and in a very short temper. It seems she'd been on the back lot shooting a shanty-town scene with Joel McCrea. Dressed as a boy, she'd had her hair tucked up under a cap all day and wore no makeup. She was tired and hungry, and in need of liquid refreshment. At that hour, I could only offer some rather weak, cold coffee.

"While she was being made up and her hair was being combed out, she kept up a steady stream of complaints. Finally she emerged and I stood back in awe. She was perfectly lovely, although her temper was not. She angrily blew her 'peek-a-boo bang' back from her right eye and demanded: 'Well, where do you want me?' I indicated the divan and placed a soothing swing record on the player. I took several poses with the hair bang in place, then I said, 'Why don't you just lie down on the couch and rest a moment?' I asked the hairdresser to comb out her long blond hair over the side of the divan. With the soothing music and her back in a comfortable position, she was almost asleep by the time I was ready to resume shooting. With the bulb in my hand, I said: 'Hi!' As she opened her eyes, I pressed the bulb. The look—which the public thought was extremely sexy—was caused not by passion, but by fatigue."

Veronica Lake with her "peek-a-boo" hair style combed out of her eye. 1941.

Maria Montez

Maria Montez. 1941.

Maria Montez, née Maria de Santo Silas, was born in the Dominican Republic. She was usually cast as an exotic femme fatale in such diversified locations as Rio, Hawaii, Tahiti, Baghdad, Sudan, Tangier, or Atlantis.

"I hauled my trusty old white bear rug out of the closet," Hurrell recalls, "for a shot of Maria that would appear in *Esquire*. She was vivacious in much the same way as Lupe Velez, but she didn't have a great deal of spontaneity. I played Spanish records, and when she came out of the dressing room in a revealing satin negligee trimmed in leopard fur, I matter-of-factly asked her to recline on the rug on the floor so she could look up into the camera. This maneuver had to be accomplished delicately, because of the unusual position. But she laughed and complied. This angle is extremely flattering in all respects but one—the bosom flattens out. To correct the pose, I always asked the subject to slightly cross her arms. I talked my usual mumbo jumbo, then just before I pressed the bulb, I said, 'Tiger!' and got the shot just before she broke up. Her humor was infectious and we both laughed so much that we couldn't repeat the pose and I had to be content with straight shots."

Lupe Velez

Lupe Velez, born Guadeloupe Velez de Villalobos in Mexico in 1908, made her film debut at the age of nineteen in *The Gaucho* in 1927. She had appeared in both dramatic and comedy roles, but was mainly known for her "Mexican Spitfire" series.

Lupe Velez. 1941.

"Lupe was exuberant to the point of hysteria," recalls Hurrell. "Whoever at RKO first cast her as the Mexican Spitfire knew what he was doing. She was a riot from the word go. Her delicate beauty was in complete contrast to her rowdy personality. My usual nervous intensity was no match for her; she could make me look like a featherweight with her antics. I always sent out for the latest Mexican recordings, and since she'd hum right along with the lyrics, I got some responsive stuff. She also had a penchant for bracelets, diamonds, rubies, and emeralds. She would often come into the studio with *both* arms loaded down."

Joseph Cotten

Joseph Cotten had been a success on Broadway in several plays, including *The Philadelphia Story* in 1939 opposite Katharine Hepburn. A member of the Orson Welles Mercury Theatre, he came to Hollywood in 1940 to play Jedediah Leland in *Citizen Kane*. He was thirty-six years old. His performance was memorable.

"Joe was free-lancing when I first shot him," Hurrell says, "and his agents were trying to wangle a motion-picture contract. He came into the Rodeo studio with Jerry Asher, a publicity man whom I'd known since the Warner days. 'Make it good,' he said, 'I'm going to peddle the photographs to the studios.'

"Cotten was typical of the new type of leading men of the 1940s," Hurrell says, "not overtly handsome as Robert Taylor or Charles Boyer, or as rugged as Clark Gable or Humphrey Bogart. But, he had a beautifully placed voice from his long experience in radio. I shot straight on but asked him to lower his head, which made his chin appear more prominent and his forehead less high. The glass brick background that I placed him against for the shots added a modern touch that made his wavy, sandy hair more interesting in the camera."

Joseph Cotten. 1942.

Teresa Wright, before The Pride of the Yankees. *1942.*

Teresa Wright

In 1941, Teresa Wright, twenty-three, fresh from the *Life with Father* Broadway production, was brought to the Samuel Goldwyn studios to play the sixteen-year-old daughter in *The Little Foxes.* Her third film was *The Pride of the Yankees* in 1942 with Gary Cooper, the moving story of baseball king Lou Gehrig and his understanding wife. Hurrell was shooting the principals for poster art when Goldwyn dropped into the gallery for a moment. He indicated Teresa Wright, an all-American type. "What do you think of this new gull? Can you make her sexy?"

Reminded of the first Norma Shearer sitting, Hurrell smiled: "I'll try." He selected a white chiffon gown with ostrich plumes from wardrobe and cautioned the fitter to see that the garment was properly taken in in the right places.

"Teresa arrived straight from makeup and hairdressing, looking uncomfortable in the gown. It was a damp day and the limp feathers drooped as she walked." Hurrell turned up the heat ten degrees, and placed her on a couch in a reclining position. He played soft music and pressed the bulb a few times. While she was rather bland offscreen, she did have a certain intensity that came over in the camera. He fanned the plumes, which were curling properly in the heat, then scowled at her. She pouted and he made a shot. He sang with the music, making up new lyrics and she responded with a slight smile. He exposed a few more plates. When the proofs came back, Teresa Wright looked like a sultry siren instead of the typical "girl next door."

Columbia

In late 1942, Robert Taplinger called Hurrell. Taplinger had moved from Warner Bros. to Columbia Pictures, and now he had an offer to make. Would Hurrell come and work for him there?

Hurrell thought over the offer very thoroughly. Columbia Pictures had gained in reputation and was no longer considered "poverty row." But Harry Cohn, in charge of the studio, was an irascible, difficult executive, who often measured a film's worth literally by the seat of his pants. When he began to fidget, he knew that audiences would also begin to fidget.

"But experience had taught me," Hurrell comments, "that portrait men were pretty much left alone. As long as a cordial relationship was maintained with the publicity and ad departments, there was usually no conflict with the production people. And at that point, I had clout—and no one appreciated clout more than Harry Cohn. So I agreed.

"The still gallery was located below street level, beneath makeup and hairdressing. The place was barely adequate—a cubicle compared to the galleries at Fox or Warner's. I had only been there a short time when Cohn popped his head in the door one morning and glanced over the scenery I was setting up. He did a double take at the charming nude picture of a girl on the wall. I was fond of the photograph, which was very subtly lighted and posed. He charged into the room like a Brahma bull, the riding crop that was seldom out of his hands beating a tempo on his right thigh. 'What's this?' he demanded, ogling the photograph.

" 'As you can see, Mr. Cohn, it's a picture.'

" 'A *nude* picture. Take it down. Take it down at once. We may have children in here, or visitors. For God's sake, take it down!' He waited impatiently, tapping his thigh with the crop, while I removed the photograph. Then he strode out, head held high, hands in back of him, holding the crop over his buttocks."

Hurrell received several outside magazine assignments and was grateful for the extra money, because his marriage was breaking up, and he

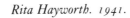
Rita Hayworth. 1941.

was in the process of an expensive divorce. Financially, he was back where he had started fifteen years before.

Rita Hayworth

"Rita had grown up in the business," Hurrell relates, "She was a member of the Cansino family of dancers and had made a lot of 'B' pictures before she got a break in big productions. While at Warner's for *The Strawberry Blonde*, she had played second fiddle. Now she was being groomed as a glamour personality in her own right. We created a new image. She had a nice personality, but could be rather subdued. But if she was experiencing a case of the blahs, all I had to do was place a tango, samba, or rumba record on the phonograph, and her spirits would perk up and the pot would start to boil.

"My first run-in with Harry Cohn happened over a layout I was doing of Rita for *Esquire*. I needed several revealing nightgowns for her, but the selection of negligees in wardrobe were very ordinary. I went over to Western Costume on Melrose Avenue and found exactly what I needed for thirty dollars' rental. A morning or so later, I received a summons to Cohn's office. He was seated at his desk, being shaved by a barber holding a long, straight razor. Production men were seated on either side of the room waiting for a meeting. It was obvious that I was getting the 'treatment.'

" 'I hear,' Cohn said loudly, 'that you've been down to Western renting costumes.'

" 'That's right.'

" 'Why? We've got a great wardrobe department right here.'

"He got up and shook his finger at me, while the barber stood two paces behind. When Cohn sat down again, the barber resumed his work.

" 'Frankly, I couldn't find anything suitable for the Hayworth layout. I need revealing stuff and Western has the best.'

" 'Yeah? Well, I don't think so!' Cohn got up, picked up his riding crop, and started to pace in front of his desk. The executives looked embarrassed.

" 'Well, I can't see spending thirty bucks when we're loaded with perfectly photographable gowns right here.'

" 'Yes, sir.' He flicked his right thigh rhythmically with the crop and it looked for a moment as if he was going to hit *my* thigh, which, of course, was exactly the mental impression he wanted to convey.

" 'If I were you,' he shouted, his face red, 'I'd use our own wardrobe. Savvy?'

" 'Yes, sir.'

" 'Okay, no sense your wasting more of my time.' He sat down, turned his swivel chair so that his back was toward me, and the barber patiently applied more lather. I was just outside the door when I heard him laughing. That was our last heated encounter. The next time I saw him on the lot, he nodded cordially and waved his riding crop at me."

Hurrell subsequently photographed Hayworth many times and created many pinup pictures that ended up pasted inside the foot lockers of servicemen all over the world. She was one of the most pliable female stars he ever photographed. The camera brought out a kind of erotic personality—an excitement both innocent and abandoned. Her figure, like Crawford's, was in perfect proportion. She could wear sleek, form-fitting gowns without being padded.

Mae West

"It had been almost ten years since I'd photographed Mae West at Paramount," recalls Hurrell, "and it would be almost thirty years before I would photograph her again. In 1943, she was on the Columbia lot to film *The Heat's On,* her first film in modern dress.

"I preferred her in costume stuff, because no one could wear clothes with quite the high style that she did. I remember after that first meeting at Paramount, she asked me to dismiss St. Hilaire from the gallery. The moment he left, she said, 'George, I want you to take some nude shots of me.' I'd been around Hollywood for quite a spell, but this was the first such request I'd had from a major celebrity. She removed her clothing and I discovered she had a beautiful body. I made the shots, she dressed and, just before she left, held out her hand and said: 'Now give me the plates, please.' Regretfully, I handed over the films, because I'd have liked one for my private collection.

"I photographed her on *The Heat's On* set, and found her to be the same witty, down-to-earth lady. The only change was that she had grown more cognizant of technical aspects. Her knowledge of lighting and camera angles was truly astonishing. Her brilliance was sometimes hidden under a rather vague manner. I'd be lulled along, shooting quickly, and she'd come up with a one-liner that would break me up.

"When I shot her again for *Myra Breckinridge* in 1969, she had the same easy style and had not forgotten how to conduct a love affair with the camera. At seventy-seven, Mae West, the only true legend in Hollywood, still had a peaches-and-cream complexion."

"I had just finished shooting Glenn Ford and Marguerite Chapman for *Destroyer,* when the mail arrived. I discovered that I had been drafted into the First Motion Picture Unit of the U.S. Army Air Force. I was to report to the Hal Roach Studios the next day.

"Two days later, given my assignment, I reported to 'Fort Roach' at five-thirty in the morning, and half an hour later found myself peeling potatoes with composer David Rose. We looked ruefully at each other, and then burst out laughing.

"I shot stills of personnel involved in training films produced by the unit." One day, he slipped away from Fort Roach early and rushed to Long Beach. In a simple justice-of-the-peace ceremony, Pvt. George Hurrell married model Phyllis Bounds.

In a few weeks, he was transferred to the Pentagon where he photographed generals. There was no gallery, no music, no madcap routines, only a series of faces, bored and uninteresting, frozen into posterity by Hurrell's magic lighting.

"In April of 1943, having reached the age where the Army no longer wanted me," Hurrell says, "I was quietly mustered out and just as quietly resumed my contract at Columbia. While I'd been in service, the Jane Russell 'haystack' photographs were creating a furor. I was requested to do more pinup work and several important magazine assignments came through. My finances were improving."

OVERLEAF LEFT: *At the time of* Goin' to Town. *1934.*

RIGHT: *As Fay Lawrence in* The Heat's On. *1943.*

FAR RIGHT: *In* Myra Breckinridge. *1970.*

179

Fanny Brice

"I photographed Fanny Brice and her alter ego, Baby Snooks, while I was in service during the early part of the war. I rented the Christie-Sheppard studios on Hollywood Boulevard for the occasion.

"Fanny was stunning in real life, and one of the best-dressed women on either coast. Her innate sense of good taste was evident in many houses that she decorated as a hobby. I shot her on an elegant couch. Since there was no phonograph, I tuned the radio to a classical-music station. I worked her into a dreamy, faraway mood, so that her inner beauty would come through. I reset my lights while she changed, and a few minutes later, I heard her croon, 'Hel-lo, kid!' I looked up to see Baby Snooks peeking around a scenery flat. I switched the radio to a boogie-woogie number, and she danced, pirouetted, and clowned as I shot plate after plate.

"I was rounding up my gear when she appeared once more—in street clothes. She extended her hand. 'Thank you, Mr. Hurrell,' she said formally, then out of the side of her mouth came her Baby Snooks voice, 'Good-bye, Georg-ie!' "

You Were Never Lovelier

Hurrell was summoned to the set of *You Were Never Lovelier*, to photograph Rita Hayworth and Fred Astaire performing a dance routine. There were a number of disconcerting problems. In the first place, he seldom shot "action" since realistic movement was extremely difficult to catch in an 8 x 10 camera. Focusing was almost impossible, and it was crucial that the bodies be caught in a graceful position, and at the same time faces must not be obscured. The camera was set up on the stage, and he took a number of shots, which, as he had feared, had a static look. He discarded the prints and walked about the set, seeking inspiration. Suddenly, he knew what was wrong. Of course, it was the *angle!*

He asked for a large, commodious platform to be built on the roof of the building in which the gallery was located. The session was scheduled for early afternoon, so that natural light would illuminate the dancers. A

TOP: *Fanny Brice as Baby Snooks. 1943.*

BOTTOM: *Fanny Brice. 1943.*

Fred Astaire and Rita Hayworth in You Were Never Lovelier. *1943.*

8 x 10 view camera was set up below the scaffolding, and the lens was focused sharply on a chalk mark on the platform. A "playback" machine was installed, and as the music sailed forth, Astaire and Hayworth went through their paces against a wide expanse of blue sky. They worked out the dance routine so that both were facing the camera as the chalk mark was reached. Hurrell shot plate after plate at two hundred fiftieth of a second—in those days possible only in natural sunlight. The shots were used widely by the studio in advertising, and established a precedent and created a new high in dance photography.

His Columbia contract was up. Hurrell was able to help see that Al St. Hilaire was promoted to photographer at the studio.

Free Again

At the end of 1943, Hurrell went back to Rodeo Drive, and resumed work on his *Esquire* series and his free-lance work.

In 1946, Hurrell moved to New York for a "short" visit that would last six years. He rented a coach house at 102 Park Avenue, hung out his shingle, and started to rebuild his bankroll by fulfilling magazine commitments and working with the advertising agencies on commercial accounts.

Joan Bennett

"Joan Bennett, Constance's sister, lived with her husband, Walter Wanger, in a fourteen-room French Provincial house on Mapleton Drive in Holmby Hills," Hurrell relates. "She called me over to 'take some shots—just for me, no particular picture.' Years before she had been a blonde, but when she went brunette in the late 1930s, a whole new career opened up for her. Her black hair added dimension to her face, making her much more photogenic.

"Joan didn't have any tricks to display; she was warm and human and left direction to me. I took a few shots in her drawing room and then, since it was a sunny day, we moved out to the garden. I wanted to shoot her in natural light. A Dietrich or a Shearer would have immediately questioned me about whether the sunlight, filtering down through the trees, was casting unwanted shadows, but Joan was unconcerned. I shot her under a grape arbor with the sunlight striking an interesting pattern over her face and figure. She was delighted with the results."

Susan Hayward

Susan Hayward (Edythe Marriner) started out as an ingenue in *Girls on Probation* at Warner Bros. in 1938, and played a variety of insipid young

Joan Bennett. 1943.

things until *Reap the Wild Wind* in 1942, which changed her type. But not until *Smash-Up, the Story of a Woman* in 1946, for which she received an Academy Award nomination, was she considered for "handkerchief" pictures. After three more nominations, she finally won the award for *I Want to Live!* in 1959.

"Susie, whom I first met and photographed on the set at Paramount in 1942, was the first starlet who was openly impressed by my reputation. 'Oh, Mr. Hurrell,' she cooed, 'I'm so lucky to be photographed by you.' Frankly, I was speechless. I always did my job and counted myself fortunate that I'd been around long enough that I didn't have to scrounge around for work. I was able to calm Susie down eventually, but I had to catch her off guard to get anything interesting on film. I did it by jumping up and down a few times and mouthing a lot of gibberish. Later, I shot some sultry poses of her for *Esquire* with mood music and the whole works. Thank God, by that time she had lost her awe of me. I was only a friend on the other side of the camera."

Susan Hayward, for Esquire.
1943.

Judy Garland, for Esquire.
1944.

Judy Garland

"I only shot Judy Garland once, as one of the glamour girls in my *Esquire* series. Dressed in a pink negligee, with full makeup, she looked like a little girl in her mother's clothes. She found the getup amusing, struck impossible poses, laughed, kidded, and told amusing stories about herself. She was very vicacious and had an unexpected natural wit. When I played sweet love ballads, she finally stopped giggling long enough to strike a few dramatic attitudes. Like Harlow, she had deep-set eyes, which had to be lighted so as not to disappear. The slightly hollow cheeks I gave her took away the little-girl quality and she became seductive."

Dinah Shore. 1944.

Dinah Shore

Dinah Shore rushed into the coach house, hair and dress flying. It was a windy stormy morning. While Hurrell set up his lights, she disappeared into the dressing room, combed her hair, repaired her makeup, and a few moments later appeared at the doorway in a rather subdued mood.

"Dinah had come to Warner Bros. after I left," Hurrell relates, "to make *Thank Your Lucky Stars.*" She was a talented rather thin girl with an effervescent personality and a bubbling voice. Because she did mostly ballads, I played very hot swing music. I worked very quickly and did not try for strict glamour stuff but rather went for an uncomplicated wholesome quality. Her spontaneity, which was so evident in person, never quite came over in films, so I was not in the least surprised when she went so successfully into television, to which her warm and unpretentious manner was particularly attuned. Dinah Shore and I created our own whirlwind that day in the coach house."

Louella O. Parsons

"I'd known Louella Parson and her husband, 'Doc' Martin, for years socially," Hurrell recalls, "and was surprised when she phoned for an appointment. She was up in years even then, and had been a movie columnist since before World War I. The exact time of the first publication of her column was never known, because Lolly wouldn't admit the exact date.

"She arrived in a white lace evening gown, and from the look of her face and hair, I knew she'd had a great deal of professional help. All the technical know-how in Hollywood couldn't disguise the fact that she was quite plump, but the pose I gave her and my retoucher's pencil took care of that. I used two broads in front of the camera for fill light, crosslighted her with 1,000-watt spotlights and then backlighted the couch where she sat. She was lighted up like a Christmas tree. I sent the proofs over to her office-house on Maple Drive in Beverly Hills. Just before the holidays, I received the following wire:

I AM JUST CRAZY ABOUT THE PICTURES YOU SENT AHEAD THE ONE IN WHITE EVENING DRESS COULD I HAVE SIX BIG ONES LIKE IT FOR MY FAMILY FOR CHRISTMAS I WILL NEVER HAVE A PICTURE AS BEAUTIFUL I LOVE YOU

LOUELLA

Louella O. Parsons' portrait was retouched so heavily that there was very little emulsion left on the film. 1950.

Hurrell was caught in yet another change in Hollywood: *television* was the new panic word at the motion-picture studios. Old regimes were tottering and the influx of young production people and inexperienced players were creating a new and rather disturbing milieu. Older stars, photographed over the years, were no longer a powerful influence over the industry. Runaway production was rampant; movie companies were shooting pictures in all parts of the world. The Hollywood that he knew was dead; it was time to move on.

In 1954, he left Rodeo Drive and headed for New York for a two-year stint with the J. Walter Thompson Agency, an advertising firm for which he had worked off and on for a number of years. His divorce from his second wife became final, and in 1955, he married Betty Willis in Elton, Maryland. He finished his contract with Thompson, then moved to Connecticut. A year later, he was back in Laguna Beach, in a studio that was the epitome of luxury compared to his modest digs thirty years before. "The only thing the studios had in common," Hurrell laughs, "was a skylight!"

In 1958, he set up a television-commercial production company with Disney Studios in Burbank and functioned as a producer, director, and occasional cinematographer. Kellogg products, Max Factor, and Sunkist were big accounts.

Walt Disney. 1958.

Ann Sheridan

Ann Sheridan had left Warner Bros. in 1948 after *Silver River* with Errol Flynn, and was now traveling the perilous route of free-lancing. She called for an appointment at Disney. "I need some new shots, George, to let the independent producers know what I look like now."

Hurrell laughed. "You know, Annie, you're more beautiful than you were five years ago when I shot you last."

"Yeah?" She replied. "Remember, I'm still the kid from Denton, Texas, don't kid me."

The proofs turned out splendidly, and when he showed them to Sheridan, he said, "I told you how great you looked. I don't think you need worry about being cast as Whistler's Mother quite yet!"

Ann Sheridan. 1958.

After a year at Disney producing commercials with the Disney studio overhead eating up the profits, Hurrell decided to return to free-lance photography. Although he received a few assignments at the Twentieth Century-Fox gallery—the last such facility still open—he did an about-face and turned his attention to television set work. Many of his portrait-photographer friends had retired, unable to adapt to the hectic methods of 35mm photography.

"But the change for me was not really that great," Hurrell says. "I had worked on sets since the era of *A Free Soul* in 1930. The big difference was in the change of equipment. We used hand-held, lightweight cameras and used up ten times as much film, but not every shot was perfect. Portraits were out—partly because there was no time to set up dramatic lighting for stars who had no time to pose, and partly because the style of photography had changed. A new, casual trend had become commonplace. Picture magazine stories showed stars emptying the garbage pail at the curb or whipping up hush puppies in the kitchen. The veil of mystery that had separated the stars from the public had been pierced by the naked eye of the 35mm camera. But I'd always been adaptable. I'd always created my own fast tempo while shooting, so the pressure of a television set didn't disturb me. Besides, I told myself, 'If you can't lick 'em—join 'em.' And I did."

Arlene Dahl

"Arlene Dahl," Hurrell says, "came over to Disney to be photographed for a Lux soap advertisement. She was very beautiful, with red hair and green eyes, and a complexion that was out of this world. After she posed with the bar of soap in her hand, I suggested taking a few straight shots of her. She was delighted. I changed records frequently, since she was in the mood to 'give.' She was a pleasure to shoot, but I was careful about the lighting. Her dimples were so deep that any shadow in the cheek area would take away some of her sophistication. Shirley Temple was the only other star whose dimples were so distracting, but with her it was a national pastime."

Arlene Dahl.

Julie Andrews

Julie Andrews was in preproduction work on *Star!*, the story of Gertrude Lawrence, the temperamental English performer whose greatest success had been the Broadway production of *The King and I*. Twentieth Century-Fox called Hurrell to the studio for a conference. He was asked to use his old glamour technique on a series of portraits of Andrews to be used in the film, and for publicity.

"Julie was charming, and contrary to rumor, not at all difficult," Hurrell says, "But, she had that natural aloofness that many Britishers have. She was totally absorbed by the character of Lawrence. Dressed in the various costumes of the 1920s and 1930s, she gave me dramatic attitudes effortlessly. Like Shearer, she had a patrician beauty that was very photogenic. It was unfortunate that the film did poor business, because it cost millions to shoot."

LEFT: *Julie Andrews in a production number from* Star! *1968.*

ABOVE: *Julie Andrews as Gertrude Lawrence in* Star! *1968.*

Raquel Welch

Raquel Welch was portraying the part of a show girl in *The Wild Party*, in 1975, for American International Pictures. She needed a photograph of the character as an Eva Tanguay-type to be used as a prop in the film. An appointment was made at her home in Beverly Hills for her only free day, a Sunday. She was dressed in an all-white costume when Hurrell arrived with a long roll of gray paper to be used for a backdrop. Since the interior of the house was rather dark, he suggested that natural sunlight be used. They moved to the back yard, and he commandeered a white stool for a prop and rolled out the gray paper. He used a diffusion disk on the 4 x 5 camera to give the feel of an old photograph.

The shot, subsequently published in *Time* magazine, showed Raquel Welch in a fey pose that might have been shot backstage in one of the early New York productions of the Ziegfeld Follies.

Bette Davis. 1974.

Bette Davis

The voice on the telephone was unmistakable. "George, this is Bette. I'm in town and I need some new photographs."

An appointment was set at the residence of Charles Pollock, where Bette Davis was staying at the time. "Outside of being more mature, she was exactly the same as when I'd last seen her, thirty-two years before, on the set of *The Little Foxes*," recalls Hurrell. "She needed some shots for a book jacket. After these were taken, we went upstairs, where I posed her in a lovely old sitting room. The radio was tuned to a music station, and with makeup man Gene Hibbs and hairdresser Peggy Shannon on the sidelines, we could have been back at Warner Bros.

"Bette was her usual vibrant self, full of laughter and fun. She wore a black-and-white leopard pants suit and looked as if she had just stepped out of *Vogue* magazine. 'Boy,' I said, 'that guy sure has broad shoulders!' She smiled slightly and I got my shot. We kidded around back and forth, and as I left, she took my hand and said, 'George, you haven't changed a bit!' I hadn't thought about *that*."

Television...and More Features

Each year, the television season brought a rash of new shows. Hurrell worked them all: *Gunsmoke, The Dick Powell Show, Mannix, M*A*S*H, Streets of San Francisco, Mod Squad, The Loretta Young Show, The Rookies,* and *The Donny and Marie Show.* . . .

"The one element that did not change with the various shows," Hurrell comments, "was the equipment. Still photographers use 35mm motor-driven cameras, hooded with a padded 'blimp' to muffle the sound of the motor because of the sensitive recording equipment. We can shoot while the shows are being filmed or taped. We push a button and in two minutes, we have shot a whole roll of film. We grab the action and hope for the best. We work for quantity and not quality. The publicity men feel that by shooting ten rolls of film, six or seven shots are bound to come out. It is a totally different system that takes some adjusting to.

"But a show like the *Donny and Marie* hour is great fun to work because the kids are so vivacious and have such a positive outlook. It's great to be surrounded by a slice of Americana."

Occasionally a studio would call for set work on a major motion picture. "It was the same," Hurrell smiles, "and yet not the same. The leisurely pace of filming was long gone. We seldom had time for portrait work; elaborate lighting was out. I used the existing light on the set and often shot while the picture was being filmed."

He worked on *Sergeants Three* (1962) with Frank Sinatra, Dean Martin, and Peter Lawford; *Beneath the Planet of the Apes* (1970) with Charlton Heston and James Franciscus; *Flareup* (1969) with Raquel Welch; *Che* (1969) with Omar Sharif; *Justine* (1969) with Anouk Aimee and Dirk Bogarde; *The Only Game in Town* (1970) with Elizabeth Taylor and Warren Beatty; *Mephisto Waltz* (1971) with Alan Alda, Jacqueline Bisset, and Barbara Parkins; *1776* (1972) with William Daniels and Howard Da Silva; *Dirty Little Billy* (1973) with Michael Pollard; *All the President's Men* (1976) with Robert Redford and Dustin Hoffman; and others.

Anouk Aimee in the title role of Justine. *1969.*

Dean Martin in Sergeants Three. *1962.*

Charlton Heston in Beneath
the Planet of the Apes.
1970.

*Alan Alda as Myles Clarkson
in* The Mephisto Waltz.
1971.

Bing Crosby on "The Bing Crosby Show."

Gregory Peck as guest host on "The Dick Powell Theatre" television series. 1963.

Donny and Marie Osmond on "The Donny and Marie Show." *1976.*

Michael Landon directing on location for "The Little House on the Prairie." *1976.*

Gable and Lombard

"When I read in the trade papers that Universal was filming the story of Clark Gable and Carole Lombard, with James Brolin and Jill Clayburgh, I did something I never did—I phoned the publicity man at the studio and asked to be assigned to the picture. I'd shot the original stars so often that I felt I might bring something extra to the still photographs. I was told that the picture did not have an ad budget per se, that one of their contract men was being used. I told myself not to be upset, I was just getting sentimental; and I let it go at that."

Three months later a call came through from publicity at Universal. "George, we've been looking over our collection of stills from the picture . . . and we don't have any suitable stuff for poster work . . . could you shoot some ad shots?"

Hurrell paused and swallowed a sharp retort, then asked when they wanted him at the studio. He was told that Brolin's only available time was on the following Saturday, and if the shots were taken on the lot, a union crew would be necessary, plus double time. Consequently, Hurrell rented Tom Kelley's studio in Hollywood. Brolin and Clayburgh arrived with Edith Head, clothes designer on the film, a wardrobe woman, a makeup man, and a hairdresser. Lacking a phonograph, Hurrell turned on the radio to a music station to dispel the dead silence of the studio.

"What tricks I used," Hurrell comments, "had to be done with lighting, because neither star actually resembled the original. Four hours later we finally ended the sitting. I was not entirely satisfied with the results, but Brolin had to catch a plane.

"Looking back, I know it would never have occurred to the real Gable and Lombard that a picture could be based on their lives. I'm sure they never thought they'd become that famous!"

James Brolin and Jill Clayburgh as Clark Gable and Carole Lombard in Gable and Lombard. *1976.*

Margaux Hemingway

Margaux Hemingway was in Hollywood to film *Lipstick* and Hurrell was called in to shoot publicity portraits. "I went up to her house in Santa Monica Canyon on a Sunday," Hurrell comments. "Having photographed many models over the years, I knew that I'd have to drag out my bag of tricks. Traditionally, models have been schooled not to show emotion of any kind because facial expression draws the eye to the face instead of the figure. A good mannequin hides behind a blank façade.

"Margaux was an unconventional beauty in the modern manner. After she was in focus, I yelled, 'The next stop is Altoona!' She responded and I got a shot, and I screamed, 'Once more around the park!' She reacted and I got another shot. I exposed more film, running around the camera and jumping up and down. As my own shooting tempo increased, she became more expressive and forgot she was in front of a camera. It was like the old days, but after three hours, I went home exhausted."

Margaux Hemingway. 1976.

Keith Carradine

One of the most moving moments in the film *Nashville*, occurs at a Country-and-Western bar when Keith Carradine, portraying a rising recording star, accompanies himself on the guitar and sings a plaintive song he has written and composed, "I'm Easy." The song not only advanced the plot of the picture, but also caught the imagination of the public and earned the young man an Academy Award nomination for best song of the year. Shortly before the telecast of the ceremonies, Hurrell was booked to photograph Carradine for the cover of his first L.P. record album.

"By the time of the sitting," Hurrell smiles, "Carradine had won the Oscar. I had photographed his dad, John, and his brother, David, and I was reminded of the times I had shot other famous acting families—Barrymore, Fairbanks, Bennett, and Power. Keith was rather subdued, and there was not a trace of arrogance, He was not a handsome man by conventional standards, but there was a certain down-to-earth animal quality that I knew would come over on film. I had pondered about the sitting; I was told only close-ups would be needed, but I had something else in mind. After I had shot the straight stuff, I placed Keith in the foreground and caught the silhouette of his guitar in the background."

After shooting his first album cover, Hurrell looked back over his career. He had worked with monster 8 x 10 portrait cameras in luxurious studio galleries and washed prints in modest cubbyholes; he had set up 8 x 10 view box cameras on the top of buildings and placed 16mm equipment on barbecues in back yards; he had shot thousands of photographs on spacious motion-picture sets and caught quickie shots with long 300mm lenses on motor-driven cameras while television shows were being taped. He had loaded 4 x 5 holders in closets covered with blankets to keep out the light, and thrown film into 35mm cameras in broad daylight. He had worked in every phase of photography: portrait, fashion, advertising, and television commercials. It had been a long and rewarding fifty-year pilgrimage.

A showing of Hurrell's famous Hollywood star photographs was given in an art gallery in Los Angles in March of 1976. For the catalogue, Hurrell himself summed up his career and his work:

I was trying to be something different. I came out here to be a painter. . . . To make some money, I got into photography and very quickly there was no time for more painting. But I kept using that training to do something original with my photography—my own kind of lighting and posing. The most essential thing about my style was working with shadows to design the face instead of flooding it with light.

I loved photographing the stars. There was such a dramatic quality in those days—and I was such a romantic, too. The stars were electric, full of sexual qualities, alluring. Our world was a storybook—a romantic fantasy. We were talented, we were working, we all assumed we'd make money, so we didn't worry and fret about it like they do today . . . we were too busy being alive.

We were children of the gods. . . .

Technical Data

The technical data for each photograph is given in the following form:

PAGE   SUBJECT / LOCATION
NUMBER CAMERA, LENS
          FILM   APERTURE, EXPOSURE TIME
          LIGHTING
          PHOTOGRAPH SOURCE

l. = left, r. = right, t. = top, b. = bottom

---

jacket Loretta Young and Tyrone Power / 20th Century-Fox set
8x10 view, 16"
Super-X   f/22, ½ sec
750 W overhead boom light on her face and his hair; 750 W spotlight from camera as fill light; 1000 W on floor on b.g.
Twentieth Century-Fox photograph.

First Shots
Ramon Novarro / Barnes' estate
8x10 view, 16"
Super-X   f/8, ½ sec
Natural light, Novarro in shade, with sun coming from rear, creating strong highlights.

5 Ramon Novarro / M.G.M. gallery
Eastman Studio 8x10, 18" portrait
Super-X   f/8, one sec
500 W spotlight on face; 500 W floodlight on b.g.
M.G.M. photograph.

9 Norma Shearer / LaFayette P. Pl. studio
8x10 view, 14" Verito
Super-X   f/16, 2 sec
Approx. 500 W arc lamp as front keylight; 500 W spotlight from rear to touch up hair.
Photograph from the Allan Smith collection.

M.G.M.
15 Lon Chaney / M.G.M. gallery
Eastman Studio 8x10, 16"
Super-X   f/16, one sec
Broad front light; two 500 W spotlights, one right, one left; 500 W spotlight on floor next to camera creating shadow on b.g.
M.G.M. photograph.

16(l.) Greta Garbo / M.G.M. gallery
Eastman Studio 8x10, 16"
Super-X   f/16, one sec
500 W spotlight from side; broad in front of camera for fill light.
M.G.M. photograph.

16(r.) Greta Garbo / M.G.M. gallery
Eastman Studio 8x10, 16"
Super-X   f/16, one sec
750 W boom light; broad in front of camera for fill light.
M.G.M. photograph.

17 Greta Garbo / M.G.M. gallery
Eastman Studio 8x10, 16"
Super-X   f/16, one sec
Natural light from skylight.
M.G.M. photograph.

---

18 Greta Garbo / M.G.M. gallery
Eastman Studio 8x10, 16"
Super-X   f/16, ½ sec
Natural light from skylight.
M.G.M. photograph, from the Allan Smith collection.

19 Greta Garbo / M.G.M. gallery
Eastman Studio 8x10, 16"
Super-X   f/16, one sec
Two 500 W spotlights, one from front of camera, one from left.
M.G.M. photograph, from the Allan Smith collection.

20 Greta Garbo / M.G.M. gallery
Eastman Studio 8x10, 16"
Super-X   f/16, ½ sec
750 W overhead boom from rear on hair; 750 W keylight from right side of camera; 500 W floodlight for fill.
M.G.M. photograph.

22 John Gilbert / M.G.M. gallery
Eastman Studio 8x10, 16"
Super-X   f/16, one sec
750 W spotlight from left of camera.
M.G.M. photograph.

23 Irving Thalberg / porch, Thalberg beach house 8x10 view camera, 16″ Super-X f/16, ½ sec Natural sunlight. M.G.M. photograph.	

30(t.) Wallace Beery / M.G.M. gallery
Eastman Studio 8x10, 16″
Super-X   f/16, one sec
500 W spotlight from front of camera; 500 W spotlight from right floor.
M.G.M. photograph.

36 Helen Hayes / on the set
8x10 view, 16″
Super-X   f/16, 1 sec
1000 W spotlight from rear hitting hair and flowers; 500 W spotlight on b.g.; 500 W from front of camera for fill light on face.
M.G.M. photograph.

24(l.) Norma Shearer / on the set
8x10 view, 16″
Super-X   f/16, one sec
1000 W spotlight from front on her figure; two 1000 W spotlights overhead, rear, one right, one left.
M.G.M. photograph.

30(b.) Wallace Beery / Mines Field
8x10 view, 16″
Super-X   f/32, ½ sec
Natural light, silver reflector from left filling shadows on face and clothing.
M.G.M. photograph.

38 Alfred Lunt and Lynn Fontanne / M.G.M. gallery
Eastman Studio 8x10, 16″
Super-X   f/16, one sec
Broad front fill light; 500 W crosslight on both faces; 750 W boom light from rear, lighting hair; broad on b.g.
M.G.M. photograph.

24(r.) Norma Shearer / on the set
8x10 view, 16″
Super-X   f/8, ½ sec
1000 W overhead spotlight behind her, touching hair, shoulders and table; 750 W spotlight from camera for fill light; 750 W flood on b.g.
M.G.M. photograph.

31(t.) Bert Lahr / *Flying High* set
8x10 view, 16″
Super-X   f/16, one sec
1000 W spotlight from front; 1000 W spotlight, left, cross lighting from rear, touching girls' knees; 750 W spotlight from right, highlighting girls' hair and backs (plank extends piano top for girls).
M.G.M. photograph.

39 Hedda Hopper / M.G.M. gallery
Eastman Studio 8x10, 16″
Super-X   f/16, ½ sec
750 W boom light touching hair and shoulders; 750 W in front of camera.
M.G.M. photograph.

25 Norma Shearer / *Wimpole St.* set
8x10 view, 16″
Super-X   f/16, one sec
1000 W cross lighting from left; 1000 W overhead from rear, lighting hair; broad from camera for fill light.
M.G.M. photograph.

31(b.) Jimmy Durante / M.G.M. gallery
Eastman Studio 8x10, 16″
Super-X   f/16, one sec
750 W boom light overhead; broad from camera for fill light.
M.G.M. photograph.

40 Jackie Cooper / M.G.M. set
8x10 view, 16″
Super-X   f/8, ½ sec
750 W spotlight from right front; 1000 W overhead back light.
M.G.M. photograph.

26(l.) Marie Dressler / *Dinner at Eight* set
8x10 view, 16″
Super-X   f/8, ½ sec
1000 W overhead front light; 750 W overhead spotlight, touching up hair and hand.
M.G.M. photograph, from the Robert Wade Chatterton collection.

32(t.) Robert Montgomery / M.G.M. gallery
Eastman Studio 8x10, 16″
Super-X   f/16, one sec
1000 W spotlight from front of camera; 1000 W crosslight from right of camera.
M.G.M. photograph.

42 Jean Harlow / Sunset Blvd. gallery
8x10 view, 16″
Super-X   f/16, one sec
750 W overhead boom light, broad used for fill light.
M.G.M. photograph.

26(r.) Marie Dressler / M.G.M. gallery
Eastman Studio 8x10, 16″
Super-X   f/8, ½ sec
Floodlight from front: 500 W crosslight from side, lighting face.
M.G.M. photograph.

32(b.) Robert Montgomery / Polo field
8x10 view, 16″
Super-X   f/32, ½ sec
Natural light.
M.G.M. photograph.

44 Jean Harlow / at her home
8x10 view, 16″
Super-X   f/16, one sec
Two 750 W photofloods on floor, either side of fireplace; 750 photoflood from front of camera for fill light.
M.G.M. photograph.

27 Marie Dressler / at her home
8x10 view, 16″
Super-X   f/8, ½ sec
Two 500 W floodlights, from front, one slightly closer to her; natural light from b.g. window.
M.G.M. photograph.

34 Leslie Howard / M.G.M. gallery
Eastman Studio 8x10, 16″
Super-X   f/8, ½ sec
500 W floodlight in front of camera as keylight; 750 W boom light overhead; 1000 W floodlight on right side of b.g.
M.G.M. photograph.

45(l.) Jean Harlow / Bullocks Wilshire store
8x10 view, 16″
Super-X   f/16, one sec
Two photofloods, both 750 W, from either side of camera.

30(l.) Wallace Beery / M.G.M. gallery
Eastman Studio 8x10, 16″
Super-X   f/16, ½ sec
Two 1000 W spotlights, one right, one left; 500 W spotlight in front of camera for fill.
M.G.M. photograph.

35 Robert Young / M.G.M. gallery
Eastman Studio 8x10, 16″
Super-X   f/8, ½ sec
750 W spotlight from left side of camera hitting coat.
M.G.M. photograph.

45(r.) Jean Harlow / at her home
8x10 view, 16″
Super-X   f/16, one sec
750 W overhead boom light, hitting her head from rear; 750 photoflood on right near floor; 750 W photofloods from camera.
M.G.M. photograph.

46   Jean Harlow / M.G.M. set
8x10 view, 16″
Super-X   f/16, one sec
1000 W spotlight from front of camera for keylight; 1000 W lamp overhead, hitting hair and dress; 500 W spotlight from right, cross lighting part of dress.
M.G.M. photograph.

47   Jean Harlow / on the set
8x10 view, 16″
Super-X   f/16, one sec
1000 W spotlight for keylight; 500 W on b.g.
M.G.M. photograph.

48   Johnny Weissmuller / M.G.M. gallery
Eastman Studio 8x10, 16″
Super-X   f/16, one sec
1000 W spotlight overhead front.
M.G.M. photograph.

49   Johnny Weissmuller / on the set
8x10 view, 16″
Super-X   f/16, one sec
Two 1000 W spotlights cross lighting figure; broad on b.g.; broad from front of camera front lighting figure.
M.G.M. photograph, from the John Kobal collection.

50   Maureen O'Sullivan / M.G.M. gallery
Eastman Studio 8x10, 16″
Super-X   f/8, ½ sec
500 W spotlight on face; 1000 W spotlight overhead rear; 500 W spotlight on b.g.
M.G.M. photograph.

51   Myrna Loy / M.G.M. set
8x10 view, 16″
Super-X   f/16, one sec
1000 W spotlight from left from stair; 1000 W spotlight used as flood.
M.G.M. photograph.

54   John Barrymore / *Grand Hotel* set
8x10 view, 16″
Super-X   f/16, one sec
1000 W keylight from camera; 1000 W backlight; 1000 W spotlight on b.g.
M.G.M. photograph.

55(t.)   John and Lionel Barrymore / *Grand Hotel* set
8x10 view, 16″
Super-X   f/16, one sec
1000 W lamp, flooding from camera as keylight; 1000 W spotlight from left of camera; 1000 W spotlight backlight on top of heads.
M.G.M. photograph.

55(b.)   Lionel Barrymore / set
8x10 view, 16″
Super-X   f/8, ½ sec
500 W spotlight on right; broad fill light.
M.G.M. photograph.

56   Wallace Beery / *Grand Hotel* set
8x10 view, 16″
Super-X   f/16, one sec
1000 W overhead toplight from rear; 500 W from back on left floor, lighting side of head; 1000 W lamp from right side of camera; broad fill light.
M.G.M. photograph.

57   Joan Crawford / *Grand Hotel* set
8x10 view, 16″
Super-X   f/16, one sec
100 W overhead backlight; 500 W front keylight.
M.G.M. photograph.

58(b.)   Joan Crawford and John Barrymore / *Grand Hotel* set
8x10 view, 16″
Super-X   f/16, one sec
1000 W overhead backlight; broad fill light, filling shadows; 1000 W spotlight on b.g.
M.G.M. photograph.

58(t.)   Joan Crawford and Wallace Beery / *Grand Hotel* set
8x10 view, 16″
Super-X   f/16, ½ sec
750 W spotlight in front of camera; 1000 W overhead spotlight.
M.G.M. photograph.

59   Greta Garbo and John Barrymore / *Grand Hotel* set
8x10 view, 16″
Super-X   f/8, ½ sec
750 W boom light from camera used as fill light; 1000 W spotlight hitting both heads; 500 W spotlight right rear lighting his figure; broad on b.g.
M.G.M. photograph.

60   Ethel Barrymore / in her garden
8x10 view, 16″
Super-X   f/32, ½ sec
Natural light filtering through trees.
M.G.M. photograph.

61   Barrymore family / Ethel Barrymore's garden
8x10 view, 16″
Super-X   f/32, ½ sec
Natural light; two silver reflectors, one left, one right.
M.G.M. photograph.

63   Joan Crawford / M.G.M. gallery
8x10 view, 16″
Super-X   f/8, ½ sec
750 W boom light from left side; broad as flood; 750 W overhead boom from rear on hair.
M.G.M. photograph.

64   Joan Crawford / M.G.M. set
8x10 view, 16″
Super-X   f/16, one sec
1000 W spotlight from left; 750 W overhead boom light, hitting top of head; 750 W spotlight cross lighting from right, hitting dress from elbows down.
M.G.M. photograph.

65   Joan Crawford / M.G.M. set
8x10 view, 16″
Super-X   f/16, one sec
1000 W floodlight behind translucent staircase to help silhouette her body; 1000 W overhead backlight; 750 W spotlight directly behind her on top step; 1000 W spotlight in front of camera used as key and fill light.
M.G.M. photograph.

66   Joan Crawford / M.G.M. set
8x10 view, 16″
Super-X   f/16, one sec
750 W spotlight from left, overhead.
M.G.M. photograph.

67   Joan Crawford / M.G.M. set
8x10 view, 16″
Super-X   f/16, one sec
750 W spotlight from right side, overhead; broad fill light.
M.G.M. photograph.

69   Douglas Fairbanks, Jr. / at his home
8x10 view, 16″
Super-X   f/8, ½ sec
750 W spotlight on face as keylight; 500 W photoflood on b.g.
M.G.M. photograph.

71   Clark Gable and Joan Crawford / M.G.M. set
8x10 view, 16″
Super-X   f/16, ½ sec
1000 W overhead spotlight; 1000 W spotlight from camera.
M.G.M. photograph.

72   Clark Gable and Joan Crawford / M.G.M. set
8x10 view, 16″
Super-X   f/8, ½ sec
2000 W spotlight from camera.
M.G.M. photograph.

73 Clark Gable / M.G.M. gallery
Eastman Studio 8x10, 16″
Super-X   f/16, one sec
750 W boom light, overhead from rear; 750 W spotlight hitting right side of face; broad from camera as fill light; broad on b.g.
M.G.M. photograph.

74 Clark Cable / M.G.M. gallery
Eastman Studio 8x10, 16″
Super-X   f/8, ½ sec
750 W spotlight from right; broad from left side of camera.
M.G.M. photograph.

75 Laurence Olivier / M.G.M. gallery
Eastman Studio 8x10, 16″
Super-X   f/16, one sec
1000 W spotlight on floor, right side of camera; 1000 W spotlight on floor, left side of camera.
M.G.M. photograph.

76 Marion Davies / M.G.M. gallery
Eastman Studio 8x10, 16″
Super-X   f/8, ½ sec
750 W spot keylight from camera; 750 W overhead boom light on hair; broad on b.g.
M.G.M. photograph.

Independent
81 Constance Bennett / Sunset Blvd. studio
8x10 view, 16″
Super-X   f/16, ½ sec
750 W spotlight on hair; 500 W lamp on face; 750 W spotlight on b.g.
RKO photograph.

83 Luise Rainer / at her home
8x10 view, 16″
Super-X   f/16, ½ sec
Natural light from b.g. window; 750 W spotlight on face from camera.
M.G.M. photograph.

85(l.) Rosalind Russell / Rodeo Dr. studio
8x10 view, 16″
Super-X   f/16, ½ sec
750 W boom light on hair; 500 W spotlight on right side of face; 500 W fill light from camera.
From a reproduction.

85(r.) Rosalind Russell / M.G.M. set
8x10 view, 16″
Super-X   f/16, ½ sec
1000 W spotlight overhead.
M.G.M. photograph.

86 Adrian / at his apartment
8x10 view, 16″
Super-X   f/16, ⅕ sec
750 W spotlight on left side; 1000 W lamp on floor on b.g.
M.G.M. photograph.

87 Tallulah Bankhead / Sunset Blvd. studio
8x10 view, 16″
Super-X   f/16, ½ sec
750 W overhead boom light on face; 1000 W on floor on b.g.

88 Gloria Vanderbilt / at her home
8x10 view, 16″
Kodachrome   f/8, ⅕ sec
Two 500 W photofloods, one on left side of camera, one on right side of camera.
From a color reproduction.

90(t.) William Powell / Sunset Blvd. studio
8x10 view, 16″
Super-X   f/16, ⅕ sec
750 W overhead boom light on head and shoulders; 750 W overhead spotlight from camera.
M.G.M. photograph.

90(b.) Robert Taylor / Sunset Blvd. studio
8x10 view, 16″
Super-X   f/16, ⅕ sec
750 W boom light on hair; 750 W spotlight from left of camera; 500 W spotlight on b.g.
M.G.M. photograph.

91 Franchot Tone / M.G.M. gallery
Eastman Studio 8x10, 16″
Super-X   f/16, ⅕ sec
750 W overhead boom light on top of head; 750 W keylight on face; 750 W lamp on b.g.
M.G.M. photograph.

92 Miriam Hopkins / Sunset Blvd. studio
8x10 view, 16″
Super-X   f/16, ⅕ sec
750 W overhead boom light on hair; 750 W spotlight from left side of camera; 1000 W spotlight on floor for b.g.
RKO photograph.

93 Charles Laughton / Sunset Blvd. studio
8x10 view, 16″
Super-X   f/16, ⅕ sec
750 W boom light on hair and hand; 500 W spotlight on face; 500 W spotlight on left, cross lighting face.

94 Elsa Lanchester / Sunset Blvd. studio
8x10 view, 16″
Super-X   f/16, ⅕ sec
750 W overhead boom light from rear; 500 W spotlight on left; two 750 W spotlights on floor, from camera, one left, one right, creating shadows on b.g.

95(t.) Spencer Tracy / M.G.M. gallery
Eastman Studio 8x10, 16″
Super-X   f/16, ⅕ sec
750 W spotlight cross lighting face from right; 750 W spotlight from camera; 500 W fill light from camera.
M.G.M. photograph.

95(b.) Spencer Tracy and Jean Harlow / M.G.M. gallery
Eastman Studio 8x10, 16″
Super-X   f/16, ½ sec
750 W boom light overhead, rear; 750 W spotlight on faces from camera.
M.G.M. photograph, from the Gunnard Nelson collection.

96 Katharine Hepburn / Rodeo Dr. studio
8x10 view, 16″
Super-X   f/16, ⅕ sec
750 W spotlight from right side of camera.
M.G.M. photograph.

97 Katharine Hepburn / Sunset Blvd. studio
8x10 view, 16″
Super-X   f/16, ⅕ sec
750 W boom light; 750 W spotlight from left on face; 1000 W lamp on floor on b.g.

99 Mary Pickford and Buddy Rogers / Sunset Blvd. studio
8x10 view, 16″
Super-X   f/16, ⅕ sec
750 W boom light on hair; 750 W spotlight on faces; 500 W fill light from left of camera; 1000 W spotlight on floor b.g.

100 Mary Pickford / at Pickfair
8x10 view, 16″
Super-X   f/16, ½ sec
Natural light from b.g. window; 750 W spotlight from left side; 500 W fill light from camera.

101 Eleanor Roosevelt / Lane home
8x10 view, 16″
Super-X   f/16, ½ sec
500 W photoflood from right; 500 W photoflood from camera as fill light.

Paramount

103 Cecil B. DeMille / Paramount gallery
Eastman Studio 8x10, 16″
Super-X   f/8, 1/5 sec
750 W keylight from left side of camera; 500
W fill light from right side of camera.
Paramount Pictures photograph.

104 Carole Lombard / Sunset Blvd. studio
8x10 view, 16″
Super-X   f/16, 1/5 sec
750 W spotlight on face, which is reflected
in mirror.

106 Marlene Dietrich / Sunset Blvd. studio
8x10 view, 16″
Super-X   f/16, 1/5 sec
750 W overhead boom light on hair and
shoulders; 750 W spotlight on face from
camera; 1000 W lamp on b.g.

108 Marlene Dietrich / Sunset Blvd. studio
8x10 view, 16″
Super-X   f/16, 1/5 sec
750 W overhead boom light from rear coming through feathers; 750 W keylight on
face from camera.

110 Claudette Colbert / Sunset Blvd. studio
8x10 view, 16″
Super-X   f/16, 1/5 sec
750 W spotlight left on face; 500 W fill light
from camera.

111 Charles Boyer / Sunset Blvd. studio
8x10 view, 16″
Super-X   f/16, 1/5 sec
750 W boom light on hair and shoulders;
750 W spotlight on face.

112 Charles Boyer / N.B.C. Studios
8x10 view, 16″
Super-X   f/16, 1/5 sec
750 W spotlight on left side of camera; 500
W fill light from camera; 1000 W on floor on
b.g.
N.B.C. photograph.

113(l.) Anna May Wong / Sunset Blvd. studio
8x10 view, 16″
Super-X   f/16, 1/2 sec
750 W spotlight on left; 750 W spotlight on
right; 500 W fill light from camera, below
lens.
Paramount Pictures photograph.

113(r.) Anna May Wong / Sunset Blvd. studio
8x10 view, 16″
Super-X   f/16, 1/5 sec
750 W boom light on face and shoulder; 750
W spotlight on b.g.
Paramount Pictures photograph.

114 Paulette Goddard / Sunset Blvd. studio
8x10 view, 16″
Super-X   f/16, 1/2 sec
750 W boom light on front part of face and
hat; 500 W fill light from camera; 1000 W
lamp on floor for b.g.
Paramount Pictures photograph.

115 Mary Martin / Paramount gallery
8x10 view, 16″
Super-X   f/16, 1/5 sec
750 W overhead boom light on hair and
shoulders; 750 W keylight from camera.
Paramount Pictures photograph.

Samuel Goldwyn

116 Samuel Goldwyn / Goldwyn gallery
8x10 view, 16″
Super-X   f/8, 1/5 sec
750 W spotlight from right side of camera;
750 W spotlight on floor by camera, creating b.g. shadow; 1000 W spotlight on left
side of b.g.
Samuel Goldwyn photograph.

117 Anna Sten / Goldwyn set
8x10 view, 16″
Super-X   f/16, 1/5 sec
750 W overhead boom light on hair and
shoulders; 750 W spotlight used as keylight
from camera; 1000 W spotlight on floor for
b.g.
United Artists-Samuel Goldwyn photograph.

118 Gary Cooper / Sunset Blvd. studio
8x10 view, 16″
Super-X   f/16, 1/5 sec
750 W boom light on hair, shoulders, and
hand; 750 W spotlight from left; 500 W spotlight from camera as fill light.

119 Gary Cooper / *Pride of the Yankees* set
8x10 view, 16″
Super-X   f/16, 1/2 sec
750 W overhead boom light on hair and
shoulders; 750 W spotlight on the right of
camera; 500 W fill light from camera; 1000
W lamp on floor for b.g.
RKO-Samuel Goldwyn photograph.

120 Sigrid Gurie / at her home
8x10 view, 16″
Super-X   f/16, 1/5 sec
750 W overhead boom used as keylight on
face and animal; 500 W fill light from camera.

122 Ronald Colman / Sunset Blvd. studio
8x10 view, 16″
Super-X   f/16, 1/5 sec
750 W spotlight from left side of camera,
hitting face and b.g.

124 Barbara Stanwyck / Sunset Blvd. studio
8x10 view, 16″
Super-X   f/16, 1/5 sec
750 W spotlight on face and shoulders.

125 Barbara Stanwyck and Gary Cooper / Goldwyn gallery
8x10 view, 16″
Super-X   f/16, 1/2 sec
750 W spotlight on faces and figures; 750 W
boom light from rear, hitting hair and legs;
1000 W lamp on b.g. floor.
Samuel Goldwyn photograph.

Twentieth Century-Fox

127 Shirley Temple / Sunset Blvd. studio
8x10 view, 16″
Super-X   f/16, 1/5 sec
750 W boom light on hair; 750 W spotlight
on left of camera.
Twentieth Century-Fox photograph, from
the Gunnard Nelson collection.

128(t.) Shirley Temple / 20th Century-Fox gallery
Eastman Studio 8x10, 16″
Super-X   f/16, 1/5 sec
750 W overhead boom light on hair and
shoulders; 750 W keylight from camera.
Twentieth Century-Fox photograph, from
the Gunnard Nelson collection.

128(b.) Shirley Temple / 20th Century-Fox gallery
Eastman Studio 8x10, 16″
Super-X   f/16, 1/5 sec
Two 750 W spotlights, cross lighting from
right and left rear; 750 W keylight from
camera.

128(r.) Bill "Bojangles" Robinson / Sunset Blvd.
studio
8x10 view, 16″
Super-X   f/16, 1/5 sec
750 W from camera on floor; 750 W spotlight from left; 1000 W floodlighting b.g. behind stairs.

130(l.) Dolores del Rio / at her home
8x10 view, 16″
Super-X   f/16, 1/2 sec
Natural light behind her from window; 750
W spotlight from camera on face and
hands.

130(r.) Dolores del Rio / Sunset Blvd. studio
8x10 view, 16″
Super-X   f/16, ¹/₅ sec
750 W spotlight from camera on face and fur.

132(l.) Sonja Henie / at her home
8x10 view, 16″
Super-X   f/16, ¹/₅ sec
750 W overhead boom light on hair; 750 W spotlight on face from left of camera; 500 W fill light from camera; 1000 W flood lamp on floor on b.g.

132(r.) Annabella / Sunset Blvd. studio
8x10 view, 16″
Super-X   f/16, ¹/₅ sec
750 W overhead boom on hair and shoulders; 750 W spotlight as keylight on left of camera.
Twentieth Century-Fox photograph.
133 See last box, page 214.

Selznick International
136 Fredric March / A Star Is Born set
8x10 view, 16″
Super-X   f/16, ¹/₅ sec
750 W boom light on hair and shoulders; 750 W keylight from camera; 500 W lamp on b.g.
United Artists-Selznick International photograph.

137 Janet Gaynor / The Young in Heart set
8x10 view, 16″
Super-X   f/16, ¹/₅ sec
750 W overhead boom light on hair and hand; 750 W spotlight as keylight from camera.
United Artists-Selznick International photograph.

138 Hedy Lamarr / at her home
8x10 view, 16″
Super-X   f/8, ¹/₅ sec
750 W floodlight as keylight on face; 750 W boom light on hair; 750 W lamp on floor to light b.g.
M.G.M. photograph.

140 Madeleine Carroll / Sunset Blvd. studio
8x10 view, 16″
Super-X   f/16, ¹/₅ sec
750 W boom light overhead on hair; 750 W spotlight over camera for fill light.
Selznick International photograph.

Warner Bros.
142 Edward G. Robinson / Warner Bros. gallery
Eastman Studio 8x10, 16″
Super-X   f/8, ¹/₅ sec
750 W spotlight on right of camera; 500 W fill light from left side of camera at lens height; 750 W on floor at left of camera.
Warner Bros. photograph.

143 Paul Muni / Warner Bros. gallery
Eastman Studio 8x10, 16″
Super-X   f/8, ¹/₅ sec
750 W lamp on right side of camera; 500 W fill light from left side of camera.

145 Bette Davis / Warner Bros. gallery
Eastman Studio 8x10, 16″
Super-X   f/8, ¹/₅ sec
750 W lamp on right side of camera; 500 W fill light from left side of camera.
Warner Bros. photograph.

146 Bette Davis / Warner Bros. gallery
Eastman Studio 8x10, 16″
Super-X   f/8, ¹/₅ sec
750 W overhead boom light on head and shoulders; 500 W keylight from over camera.

147(l.) Bette Davis / The Letter set
8x10 view, 16″
Super-X   f/8, ¹/₅ sec
750 W spotlight on right side of camera.
Warner Bros. photograph.

147(r.) Bette Davis / The Little Foxes set
8x10 view, 16″
Super-X   f/8, ¹/₅ sec
750 W overhead boom light on hair; 750 W spotlight over camera on face and arms; 1000 W floodlight behind her on b.g.
RKO-Samuel Goldwyn photograph.

148 Bette Davis / Elizabeth & Essex set
8x10 view, 16″
Super-X   f/8, ¹/₅ sec
750 W spot keylight over camera.
Warner Bros. photograph, from the Whitney Stine collection.

150(l.) Olivia de Havilland / Elizabeth & Essex set
8x10 view, 16″
Super-X   f/8, ¹/₅ sec
750 W boom light over her head; 750 W keylight from camera; 1000 W floodlight behind her on b.g.
Warner Bros. photograph.

150(r.) Errol Flynn / Elizabeth & Essex set
8x10 view, 16″
Super-X   f/16, ¹/₅ sec
750 W boom light over head on hair and shoulders; 1000 W flood on floor from right side of camera; 750 W spotlight from camera used as fill light.
Warner Bros. photograph, from the Gunnard Nelson collection.

151 Errol Flynn / Warner Bros. gallery
Eastman Studio 8x10, 16″
Super-X   f/8, ¹/₅ sec
750 W overhead boom light on hair and shoulders; 750 W spotlight from right side of camera; 500 W fill light from left side of camera.
Warner Bros. photograph.

153 Humphrey Bogart / Warner Bros. gallery
Eastman Studio 8x10, 16″
Super-X   f/11, ¹/₅ sec
750 W overhead boom light on hair; 750 W keylight over camera hitting face; 750 W spotlight on b.g.

154 Frank Capra / Warner Bros. gallery
Eastman Studio 8x10, 16″
Super-X   f/8, ¹/₅ sec
750 W lamp on profile from left; 750 W boom light touching hair and shoulders; 500 W flood from camera as fill light; 1000 W floodlight on b.g. from behind him; 750 W spotlight on floor from camera creating b.g. shadow.

155 Elsa Maxwell / Warner Bros. gallery
Eastman Studio 8x10, 16″
Super-X   f/8, ¹/₅ sec
750 W boom light on face and figure; 750 W flood on b.g.
Warner Bros. photograph, from a reproduction.

157(t.) James Cagney / Warner Bros. gallery
Eastman Studio 8x10, 16″
Super-X   f/11, ¹/₅ sec
750 W overhead boom light on hair, shoulders and hands; 750 W keylight over camera; 750 W spot behind him on b.g.
Warner Bros. photograph.

157(b.) John Garfield / on outdoor set
8x10 view, 16″
Super-X   f/22, ¹/₁₀₀ sec
Natural light.
Warner Bros. photograph.

158 Ann Sheridan / Warner Bros. gallery
Eastman Studio 8x10, 16″
Super-X   f/11, ¹/₅ sec
750 W overhead boom light on hair, hands and legs; 500 W fill light on face.
Warner Bros photograph.

160 Randolph Scott / Warner Bros. gallery
Eastman Studio 8x10, 16″
Super-X   f/8, ¹/₅ sec
750 W overhead boom light on hat and shoulders; 750 W spotlight on floor, right side of camera on face and figure; 500 W fill light from left side of camera.
Warner Bros. photograph.

161 Gilbert Roland / Warner Bros. gallery
Eastman Studio 8x10, 16″
Super-X   f/8, ¹/₅ sec
750 W flood on face from left side of camera.
Warner Bros. photograph.

162(t.) Alexis Smith / Warner Bros. gallery
Eastman Studio 8x10, 16″
Super-X   f/16, ¹/₅ sec
750 W boom light on hair, shoulders, and wrapping; 750 W keylight over camera; 600 W spotlight on left of camera on lower part of wrapping; 1000 W spotlight behind her on b.g.
Warner Bros. photograph.

162(b.) Doris Duke / Warner Bros. gallery
Eastman Studio 8x10, 16″
Super-X   f/8, ¹/₅ sec
750 W overhead boom light on hair; 750 W spotlight from left side of camera as keylight.

The Waldorf and Rodeo Drive
164 Helena Rubenstein / at her apartment
8x10 view, 16″
Super-X   f/8, ¹/₅ sec
500 W photoflood overhead on hair and shoulders; 1000 W photoflood from camera as keylight.

166(t.) Jane Russell / Rodeo Dr. studio
8x10 view, 16″
Super-X   f/16, ¹/₅ sec
750 W boom light on hair and legs; 1000 W spotlight from left of camera; 500 W fill light from camera; 750 W lamp behind her on b.g.
RKO photograph.

166(b.) Jane Russell / Rodeo Dr. studio
8x10 view, 16″
Super-X   f/16, ¹/₅ sec
1000 W lamp from right of camera; 1000 W from left of camera; 750 W fill light from camera.
RKO photograph.

167 Jane Russell / Coach House studio
8x10 view, 16″
Super-X   f/16, ¹/₅ sec
750 W boom light on face and figure; 750 W spotlight on b.g. behind her.
RKO photograph.

168(l.) Gene Tierney / 20th Century-Fox gallery
8x10 view, 16″
Super-X   f/22, ½ sec
1000 W spotlight on left side of camera.
From a color reproduction.

168(r.) Gene Tierney / Rodeo Dr. studio
8x10 view, 16″
Super-X   f/8, ¹/₅ sec
750 W boom light on hair; 750 W keylight above camera on face.
United Artists photograph.

169 Betty Grable / 20th Century-Fox gallery
8x10 view, 16″
Kodachrome   f/8, ¹/₅ sec
750 W overhead boom light on hair and hands; 1000 W spotlight from left of camera lighting figure; 750 W floodlight used as fill, from right side of camera.
From a color reproduction.

170 Veronica Lake / Rodeo Dr. studio
8x10 view, 16″
Super-X   f/16, ¹/₅ sec
750 W lamp from right side of camera on hair and face; 750 W behind her on b.g.
Paramount Pictures photograph.

171 Maria Montez / Rodeo Dr. studio
8x10 view, 16″
Super-X   f/16, ¹/₅ sec
750 W spotlight on floor at right side of camera; 500 W fill light from left of camera.
Universal Pictures photograph.

172 Lupe Velez / Rodeo Dr. studio
8x10 view, 16″
Super-X   f/16, ¹/₅ sec
750 W overhead boom light on face and shoulders; 750 W lamp behind her on b.g.
RKO photograph.

173 Joseph Cotten / Rodeo Dr. studio
8x10 view, 16″
Super-X   f/16, ¹/₅ sec
750 W overhead boom light on hair and shoulders; 750 W keylight from camera; 750 W floodlight behind glass b.g.

174 Teresa Wright / Goldwyn gallery
8x10 view, 16″
Super-X   f/16, ¹/₅ sec
1000 W spotlight from right of camera; 500 W fill light from left of camera; 1000 W spotlight on b.g. behind her.
RKO-Samuel Goldwyn photograph.

Columbia
176 Rita Hayworth / Columbia gallery
8x10 view, 16″
Super-X   f/16, ¹/₅ sec
750 W spotlight on left side of camera on hair and pillow; 750 W spotlight from left side of camera on face.
Columbia Pictures photograph.

180 Mae West / Paramount gallery
8x10 view, 16″
Super-X   f/16, ¹/₅ sec
750 W boom light overhead from right of camera on face and figure; 500 W spotlight from right rear.
Paramount Pictures photograph, from the John Kobal collection.

181(l.) Mae West / Columbia gallery
8x10 view, 16″
Super-X   f/16, ¹/₅ sec
750 W spotlight from left side of camera on face and hands; 1000 W spotlight behind her on b.g.
Columbia Pictures photograph.

181(r.) Mae West / *Myra Breckinridge* set
4x5 Speed Graphic, 8″
Royal Pan   f/8, ¹/₅₀ sec
750 W lamp from right side of camera; 500 W fill light from camera.
Twentieth Century-Fox photograph.

182(t.) Fanny Brice / Christie-Sheppard studios
8x10 view, 16″
Super-X   f/16, ¹/₅₀ sec
750 W boom light overhead; 750 W spotlight on floor right of camera; 500 W on floor left of camera to light legs; 500 W fill light from camera.

182(b.) Fanny Brice / Christie-Sheppard studios
8x10 view, 16″
Super-X   f/8, ¹/₅₀ sec
750 W boom light overhead on hair; 750 W keylight on face and figure; 1000 W flood behind her on b.g.

183 Fred Astaire and Rita Hayworth / Columbia roof
8x10 view, 16″
Super-X   f/11, ¹/₂₅₀ sec
Natural light from right of camera; two silver reflectors from camera for fill light; sky b.g.
Columbia Pictures photograph.

Free Again
184 Joan Bennett / at her home
8x10 view, 16″
Super-X   f/16, ¹/₅ sec
Natural light.

186 Susan Hayward / Rodeo Dr. studio
8x10 view, 16″
Kodachrome   f/8, ¹/₅ sec
750 W overhead boom light on face and shoulders; 750 W spotlight on b.g.
From a color reproduction.

187 Judy Garland / M.G.M. gallery
8x10 view, 16″
Kodachrome   f/8, one sec
1000 W spotlight from right of camera.
From a color reproduction.

188 Dinah Shore / Coach House studio
8x10 view, 16″
Super-X   f/16, ¹/₅ sec
750 W boom light on head and shoulders;
750 W keylight on face and hands; 500 W
spotlight on right b.g.

189 Louella O. Parsons / Coach House studio
8x10 view, 16″
Super-X   f/8, ¹/₅₀ sec
750 W boom light on hair, shoulders, and
gown; 500 W keylight on face and arms; 500
W spotlight cross lighting dress from right
side of camera; two broads in front of camera for fill light.

190 Walt Disney / on Disney Studio set
8x10 view, 16″
Super-X   f/11, ½ sec
Two 1000 W spotlights in b.g. for effect;
1000 W floodlight, right side of camera on
b.g.

191 Ann Sheridan / Disney studio
8x10 view, 16″
Super-X   f/11, ¹/₅ sec
750 W boom light on hair; 750 W keylight
from left of camera on face; 1000 W lamp
behind her on b.g.

193 Arlene Dahl / Disney studio
8x10 view, 16″
Super-X   f/16, ¹/₅ sec
750 W spotlight on left of camera on face;
500 W fill light from camera.
J. Walter Thompson Agency photograph.

194(l.) Julie Andrews / *Star!* set
Nikon 35mm motor-driven, 135mm.
Tri-X   f/8, ¹/₂₅₀ sec
Existing stage lights; 10K keylight on figure;
film boosted in development to ASA 800.
Twentieth Century-Fox photograph.

194(r.) Julie Andrews / 20th Century-Fox gallery
4x5 Speed Graphic, 8″
Royal Pan   f/8, ¹/₁₀₀ sec
750 W boom light on hair; 1000 W keylight
close to camera; 1000 W floodlight on b.g.
Twentieth Century-Fox photograph.

195 Raquel Welch / in her backyard
4x5 Speed Graphic, 8″
Royal Pan   f/8, ¹/₁₀₀ sec
Natural light; No. 2 diffusion disc to re-
create "old time" feeling.

196 Bette Davis / Chuck Pollock home
Mamiyaflex, 135mm.
Tri-X   f/8, ¹/₂₅ sec
Two 500 W photofloods, on each side of
camera; 500 W keylight from left of camera;
500 W floodlight from camera as fill light.

Television . . . And More Features
198(t.) Anouk Aimee / *Justine* set
Mamiyaflex, 180mm.
Tri-X   f/5.6, ¹/₁₂₅ sec
Existing stage lighting; film boosted in de-
velopment to ASA 800.
Twentieth Century-Fox photograph.

198(b.) Dean Martin / *Sergeants Three* set
Rolleiflex, 80mm.
Tri-X   f/5.6, ¹/₁₂₅ sec
Existing stage lighting; film boosted in de-
velopment to ASA 800.
United Artists photograph.

199(t.) Charlton Heston / *Beneath the Planet of the
Apes* set
Mamiyaflex, 180mm.
Tri-X   F16, ¹/₂₅₀ sec
Natural light; two silver reflectors for fill
light; film boosted in development to ASA
800.
Twentieth Century-Fox photograph.

199(b.) Alan Alda / *Mephisto Waltz* set
Mamiyaflex, 180mm.
Tri-X   f/5.6, ¹/₁₂₅ sec
Existing stage lighting; film boosted in de-
velopment to ASA 800.
Twentieth Century-Fox photograph.

200(t.) Bing Crosby / on t.v. set
Mamiyaflex, 180mm.
Tri-X   f/8, ¹/₁₂₅ sec
Existing studio lighting.
Bing Crosby Productions photograph.

200(b.) Gregory Peck / on t.v. set
Mamiyaflex, 180mm.
Tri-X   f/8, ¹/₁₂₅ sec
Existing stage lighting; film boosted in de-
velopment to ASA 800.
Four Star Productions photograph.

201(t.) Donny and Marie Osmond / *Donny & Marie*
set
Nikon 35 mm. motor-driven, 50mm.
Tri-X   f/5.6, ¹/₁₂₅ sec
Existing stage lighting.
Osbro Concerts, Inc. photograph.

201(b.) Michael Landon / *The Little House on the
Prairie* set
Nikon 35 mm. motor-driven, 50mm.
Tri-X   f/5.6, ¹/₂₅₀ sec
Natural light.
N.B.C. photograph.

203 James Brolin and Jill Clayburgh / Kelley's
Studio
Mamiyaflex, 180mm.
Tri-X   f/6.3, ¹/₁₂₅ sec
1000 W keylight from left of camera; 500 W
boom light from rear on hair; 1000 W flood-
light on b.g.
Universal Pictures photograph.

204(l.) Margaux Hemingway / at her home
4x5 Speed Graphic, 8″
Royal Pan   f/8, ¹/₁₂₅ sec
Three 500 W photofloods, one on face as
keylight, one as fill light, one on b.g.
Sygma Photo Agency photograph.

204(r.) Margaux Hemingway / at her home
4x5 Speed Graphic, 8″
Royal Pan   f/8, ¹/₁₂₅ sec
Three 500 W photofloods, one on face as
keylight, one as fill light, one on b.g.
Sygma Photo Agency photograph.

205 Keith Carradine / Kelley's Studio
4x5 Speed Graphic, 8″
Royal Pan   f/8, ¹/₁₂₅ sec
1000 W spotlight on floor, left of camera to
create shadow on b.g. and light face; 500 W
spotlight from rear, hitting hair.
Elektra/Asylum/Nonesuch Records photograph.

133 Gypsy Rose Lee/Sunset Blvd. Studio
8x10 view, 16″
Super-X   f/16, ¹/₅ sec
750 W spotlight directly over camera.
Twentieth Century-Fox photograph.

Index

Figures in italic indicate illustrations.

ACKNOWLEDGMENTS

Various editions of *The Film Daily Yearbook* and the *International Television Almanac* have been very useful as well as *The Great Movie Stars—The Golden Years* by David Shipman, the fourth edition of *The Filmgoers Companion* by Leslie Halliwell, *The Lion's Share* by Bosley Crowther, and *A Million and One Nights* by Terry Ramsaye.

W. S.